Paranormal Perspectives

The Royal Oak Investigations

The Eternal Last Call

Welcome to Paranormal Perspectives

It was important for me to develop Paranormal Perspectives for those seeking a deeper understanding of the paranormal world. This series is intended for sceptics, believers, and those who have unfathomable experiences and are often frightened by them. These books will help their understanding of what is happening to them.

The Paranormal Perspectives series will explore, in-depth, the encounters, theories, and research into incomprehensible events and how these experiences motivated remarkable individuals to delve deeper and share their extraordinary relationships of the paranormal with the world.

Paranormal Perspectives begins with eight books exploring the spectrum of metaphysical events, with insight from the UK's top ghost detective, a licensed clinical psychologist, a retired English professor, a prolific UFO investigator, a Theologian, paranormal investigators, and a writer specialising in first-hand, personal paranormal encounters.

You, too, may have had a lifetime of unearthly experiences and may wish to add to the series. Please visit 6th-books.com for further information. We look forward to hearing from you.

I hope you enjoy this series as it guides you on your quest and pulls back the veil to shine light into the unknown.

Sleep well,
G L Davies
Author of ***Haunted: Horror of Haverfordwest***

Paranormal Perspectives
Collect and read all books in the series.

One Big Box of 'Paranormal Tricks': From Ghosts to Poltergeists to the Theory of Just One Paranormal Power
by John Fraser

A Jungian Understanding of Transcendent Experiences
by Susan Plunket

Hauntings, Attachments and Ghouls
by G L Davies

Portraits of Alien Encounters Revisited
by Nigel Harry Watson

Where the Spirit Led
by Brad Burkholder

The Royal Oak Investigations
by Ashley Knibb

A Secular Look at God and the Afterlife
by J. Allan Danelek

PARA·NORMALITY: Normalising the Paranormal
by Kieran Stanislaw Mace

Paranormal Perspectives

The Royal Oak Investigations

The Eternal Last Call

by Ashley Knibb

6TH
BOOKS

London, UK
Washington, DC, USA

CollectiveInk

First published by Sixth Books, 2026
Sixth Books is an imprint of Collective Ink Ltd.,
Unit 11, Shepperton House, 89 Shepperton Road, London, N1 3DF
office@collectiveinkbooks.com
www.collectiveinkbooks.com
www.6th-books.com

For distributor details and how to order please visit the 'Ordering' section on our website.

ISBN: 978 1 917704 12 0
978 1 917704 22 9 (ebook)
Library of Congress Control Number: 2025933203

A CIP catalogue record for this book is available from the British Library.

Design: Lapiz Digital Services

UK: Printed and bound by CPI Group (UK) Ltd, Croydon, CR0 4YY
Printed in North America by CPI GPS partners

The manufacturer's authorised representative in the EU for product safety is: eucomply OÜ - Pärnu mnt 139b-14, 11317 Tallinn, Estonia, hello@ eucompliancepartner.com, www.eucompliancepartner.com

Contents

Chapter One

The Perception of Time and Movement

We sat there on the floor, facing each other, Pete and me. The entire room was dusty, with some equally dusty boxes stacked nearer to the walls. The room looked as if it had been untouched for many years, but this was unlikely the case. The ladder that had allowed us access through the standard hatch, was left in position with the hatch already open. Someone had most certainly been up in that space, where we now sat, probably within the last week.

The loft space was also situated above the first-floor bedroom where we had received many reports of strange paranormal acivity. Rachael, the landlady of the Royal Oak public house in Swanage, had told me how many people had felt trapped in this room or that the very atmosphere of the space was extremely heavy.

Oddly the previous landlady of the Royal Oak, Sharon, also told me of the unwelcome and trapped feelings that this room had provided them during their ten years at the pub. Incidentally it was Sharon and her partner that discovered a false wall which concealed the entrance to the loft space above. They removed the false wall to gain access to it. A piece of information that always troubled me as surely they meant that the room was actually concealed by a false wall, as concealing a loft entrance would not require a false wall. Perhaps this would become more understood in the future, when this space would be transformed once again.

Moonlight illuminated the loft space through the rear facing window that Saturday night in March, 2010. If anything, the space felt remarkably comfortable and not unwelcome; I certainly did not feel trapped in any shape or form. I wondered if it was the fact that it was a small space that had made others feel trapped. However, I had to rule this out at this point, as no one taking part in the investigation felt anything negative.

I made the decision that both Pete and I should attempt to call out to the purported spirits at this location but in order to gain some kind of response that would be measurable, I knew we would need a trigger object. On this occasion, I took out all I had in my pocket which happened to be my grandfather's pocket watch. The simple gold coloured time piece was something I carried with me on these paranormal investigations. My grandfather had passed away in his nineties many years previously; perhaps it was my way to connect with family. Importantly the pocket watch did not work and whilst I am sure I could get it fixed, it felt like it should remain just as it is, linked to him somehow. Even now, having the watch repaired is not an option. In fact, probably even more so now.

I placed the pocket watch between Pete and me, amongst the dust. Then I explained, loud enough for those in the room below to hear, what my intentions were at this point. We were to call out to the local spirits and ask them to move the pocket watch for us. It was an ambitious ask in reality as at that point in the 2010 investigation, we had not really received any real indication that we may receive an elaborate physical response, such as the movement of an object.

At some point I believe that Lucy, my sister Leanne's friend, who was assisting with filming the investigation, made her way up the less stable ladder. If memory serves me well, she positioned herself in the loft hatch, pointing the camera at us.

Pete and I began to call out to the spirits asking for them to show their presence by taps, raps or by possibly moving the pocket watch between us. At that point my radio appeared to click. Whilst it caught our attention and did appear to be in response to a question, it was inconclusive and failed to repeat.

However, when I tried something similar, the radio clicked again. It was around this point that Lucy had managed to get into position and began filming. Obviously as the camera recorded, the radio click stopped. As such, I have to rule this out as being paranormal.

To make the pocket watch more visible for the camera, I decided to raise its position. Moving it from the floor, I placed it on a box, still between Pete and me. We continued to call out to the spirits.

Only a few minutes later, Pete and I realised that something had changed as far as the pocket watch was concerned. The broken pocket watch had been running as normal, keeping time, for approximately the last twenty minutes. This would have been around the same time that we had started to ask for spirit to move the pocket watch.

We directed our line of questioning towards the now running pocket watch but received nothing that provided any additional information. It was extremely curious and would become one of the many cryptic forms of information that this little pub in Swanage would provide.

As we reached the end of our time in the loft space, I reached down and picked up the pocket watch, as I did so, it stopped again! It returned to its broken state, exactly as it was prior to its use as a trigger object.

There was probably a part of me that felt that it would be amazing if my grandfather's pocket watch had continued to work from that point forward. However, having an abrupt stop at exactly the point that I picked it up certainly added to this particular mystery.

It is probably important to note that at this point in my life and journey as a paranormal investigator, I was more sceptical than I am in the present day or at least less open minded. Back then, I was also focussed on debunking phenomena by finding logical explanations. My time at the Royal Oak pub would most certainly change my perception and open my mind to a wider possibility that psychical research can provide. It is more than ghosts, sprits and haunted houses. It has depth, and everyone that has an experience has a story; every place said to be haunted has many stories associated to it. The Royal Oak in Swanage and the characters I would meet there were evidence of that if nothing else.

Of course, I would be no kind of paranormal investigator if I did not explore other possibilities that might explain why the pocket watch behaved as it did.

Whilst still at the Royal Oak in 2010, I tried some obvious experiments. The first being to see if I may have accidentally wound the pocket watch as I removed it from my jeans pocket. Whilst this is possible, in every recreation I attempted, mostly the pocket watch was not successfully wound and as such did not run afterwards. In the one or two occasions when it was wound, it was an insignificant amount and ran for less than a minute. I certainly could not manage to get it to run for over twenty minutes.

When I returned home from the Royal Oak investigation, I would continue to test the pocket watch for months afterwards. I was convinced there was a logical explanation to this.

At one point, I even began to test other possibilities including magnets, the watch being close to the radio, perhaps the watch received an impact of some kind that kick started the time piece; however, no explanations presented themselves or recreated the same scenario.

As I write this, over twelve years later, with the pocket watch in front of me, I realise none of these would make the watch run for as long as it did. In fact, closer inspection of the pocket watch shows that it cannot even be wound any more.

Often as we investigate the paranormal, we have to be cautious that we do not associate too much significance to an event or experience. As that may in many circumstances bias our opinions and as such our conclusions of what actually happened or what possibly happened.

For Rachael and those that joined us on that first investigation, I am sure that the watch running was associated to the local spirits of the pub, in their opinion. They believed the local spirits were providing their ghostly interaction the best they could. In doing so, providing some evidence for me and my team to take home with us. To be fair, as there is no obvious explanation, this could be very true and a reasonable conclusion with the absence of any results from my experiments to find a logical explanation. We would, of course, begin to learn much more about the reported spirit residence of the Royal Oak in the years to come.

Leanne, my sister, had joined my team to help document the events of my paranormal investigations. We once had lofty ideas of making a television series from the footage, but the idea never really evolved. Instead, my investigations found their place as blog posts on my website (www.ashleyknibb.com) or as articles in various paranormal magazines like *Ghost Voices Magazine, Haunted Magazine* and the *Magazine of the Society for Psychical Research*. Still, back then Leanne and her friends joined and used their professional skills from television to help properly film the events. Between us, we probably have a huge library of footage from our visits. Perhaps one day that will find a better home too, rather than a box under my desk.

As Leanne was also present back in March, 2010 when Pete and I sat in that dusty loft space, I am sure that like me, once all logical possibilities were exhausted, her mind must have thought of the pocket watch's previous owner, our grandfather.

It was natural for us to consider that as the previous owner of the pocket watch our grandfather, Len Larbey, may have somehow managed to influence it; possibly as a way to communicate with us, his family. Although I do not discount this possibility, it begins to confuse me when I think it through:

why at the Royal Oak and nowhere else? In 2010, I had not read or learnt as much as I have done in the last twelve years. As such, other possibilities would become evident to me as I continued to visit the Royal Oak over the next twelve years.

So, at that point in 2010, without additional possibilities presenting themselves, I had to consider two explanations, a) a local spirit influenced the pocket watch in response to us asking them to move it, or b) a non-local spirit, namely my grandfather, influenced his old pocket watch. Also, to be clear here, the term "local spirit" refers to a spirit considered to be local or attached to the Royal Oak itself, whilst a "non-local spirit" has no such attachment.

The problem being with this "local" and "non-local" terminology in this case, may be that my grandfather as we may discover had an affiliation with Swanage. Which could mean there may actually be a reason that he too appeared to be linked to the Royal Oak. Often, I have discovered such connections are extremely loose and as such should not be considered too deeply, but there was one thing that felt oddly familiar about Swanage. This was the railway station, and the engine shed located not far from it that had a turntable. It all seemed very similar to the garden railway that my grandfather had at his house in Potters Bar, which we visited often as children. Is it possible that my own family had a connection to Swanage and maybe even the Royal Oak? That would be a bit of leap at this point.

I would later find out that my grandparents had in fact spent more than one holiday in Swanage. At this point, though, how much the seaside town meant to them and if there was a deeper connection to my family remained an unknown. Which meant a personal connection to the Royal Oak was not to be considered at this point.

Speaking of family, Pete, who had volunteered to climb the ladder into that dusty loft space, was the landlady's cousin.

At that point, back when we conducted our first official overnight investigation, I believe he lived at the pub. In fact, I think he occupied the middle bedroom on the second floor (Bedroom 4). This bedroom was on the same level as the loft space, but there was a whole room in between them and no way through without going down to the first floor.

The Royal Oak has taught me a lot about memory over the years I have been visiting the location to further my investigation. The most important thing is that its fallible. Whilst you may believe you remember something exactly as it happened, it is more likely that you do not. This is why multiple witness statements are better than one and cross-referencing those statements can lead to a true understanding of the events. However, sometimes you may only have your own experiences to go on or that of one other, but that should not mean you quickly rule them out. Oddities occur, of that I am certain, how they occur or what their source is, now that's a whole different question.

Often during my time at the Royal Oak, I have been presented with similar questions, especially by the locals and at points of high strangeness. They would ask me to provide an explanation of some weird event and when I had rattled off a few theories knowing I did not have the answer, they would provide suggestions that the pub was haunted. I had to admit, if all that weird stuff was what a haunting looked like, then perhaps it was.

Pete, like me, was fascinated by my grandfather's pocket watch running for about twenty minutes for what appeared to be no reason at all. Well, no obvious logical reason. He was a well-presented, tidy, tall professional who at that point appeared curious about the paranormal and eager to learn about our approach as investigators. Pete certainly did not present himself as having a particular belief in the spiritual aspects of this case but was open minded enough to accept various possibilities as an explanation. At that point, my knowledge of psychokinesis was limited and as such was only a loosely suggested possibility. The theory being that by suggesting the watch should move, Pete and I somehow achieved this, but only so far as making the hands move. This would be one theory that would grow more popular with me over time as I learnt more about psi and parapsychology through reading and my membership with the Society for Psychical Research (SPR).

That initial investigation provided me with more than I thought I would get but equally left me with many interesting questions. In fact, they would be questions that would lead me to join the SPR, read a great deal, talk to academics and begin to look into a few more famous cases. It could also be said that it may have enabled me to work with many others in the field, including with some overseas.

The Royal Oak case would always remain very different from others I have investigated over the years. Most of the investigations I have either run or attended have been at a location that you could consider to be public. These would range from pubs like the Royal Oak, to manor houses, museums, old hospitals, derelict theatres, prisons, forts and castles. The similarity for all these locations was that we would spend one night investigating the paranormal claims made about the places. Often as the group attending was a mix of believers, non-believers and those not so sure, we would have interesting nights where activity may be similar to that which was previously reported. Equally, we may also receive an abundance of information we could never qualify. Much of this information was either provided by the more spiritual of the group or those using divination techniques like Ouija boards or pendulums. Another more prominent source of this kind of information in more recent years was what I would class as ghost hunting gadgets or mobile phone apps.

Ghost hunting gadgets are basically anything like a measuring device or audio device that has been created for and marketed to the many ghost hunters out there. For example, the KII Meter is a small hand-held Electromagnetic Field (EMF) measuring device that has coloured LEDs that light up in reaction to more intense EMF. Many ghost hunters do not use these to measure EMF, they use them to communicate with ghosts. For all intents and purposes, a measuring device has become a divination device. Ghost hunters will ask questions into the darkness, and when the KII Meter illuminates, this is seen as interaction or answers to questions. This is all based on the unproven theory that ghosts may be able to influence EMF, as they may be comprised of energy. There is a bigger back story to this theory, but I am not sure it is totally relevant to the Royal Oak story.

The ghost hunting apps found on tablet devices and smart phones are also becoming hugely popular amongst many younger ghost hunters. Possibly because many of us are now not very far from our mobile technology, so using an app to detect or communicate with ghosts is a natural step. However, these again are not a million miles from older divination techniques. Like the aforementioned gadgets, these appear to be more aligned with spiritual approaches than good science. This is because the ghost hunters do not capture measurements and then search for patterns; they follow a more dramatic approach where responses become "evidence" even when they are inconclusive.

Obviously, we must remain open minded about these things, especially when many ghost hunters are associating them with experiences that they have had at many locations. However, we must equally evaluate those experiences and all that is captured to try and gain an understanding of the paranormal, something which I started to do at the Royal Oak back in 2010 but would continue for twelve years beyond that. Especially as the case was very different from others that I had looked into at the time.

The Royal Oak case would quickly become more like a private home investigation than one of those overnight public ghost hunts. If I am honest, looking back at my notes and approach, it began like this from the outset. However, at that point I did not fully realise how important to me the case would become. On meeting Rachael for the first time, I immediately felt a rapport with her that presented her story to me as if it was obvious fact. We sat in the pub's garden on that first meeting with Aaron my paranormal investigator friend and the one that had suggested we investigate this old pub; we discussed some of the phenomena that had been encountered. That initial meeting filled me with excitement as Rachael detailed a haunting that was something I had been searching for as I travelled up and down the country on ghost hunts. However, as all good paranormal investigators know, if it sounds too good to be true then it probably is. As such, in those early encounters and before I sat in that dusty loft space, I have to admit that I was especially sceptical of the whole situation.

However, even before our first investigation in March, 2010, we managed to spend some time interviewing a few of the locals in what was the Pool Room; now it is probably called the back bar area or even just the back room. Whilst my scepticism still remained after those interviews, I was open minded enough to accept the possibility that the Royal Oak was indeed haunted and could warrant an investigation of some sort to understand more about this old pub on the edge of Swanage. It was this that led me to return in March, 2010, to do exactly that with a good size team for the location.

There was one conditional element of the Royal Oak case that would begin to change my own perspective of the paranormal: it was the people who were involved in this particular haunting, and the parts they would play in its greater understanding. Previously during investigations of purported haunted locations, I had interviewed those available to obtain the stories of their experiences. In most case this was very much like capturing a witness statement for an accident, focussed on the event in question and what occurred. Whilst I attempted a similar approach at the Royal Oak, it felt different, it was as if I had stepped into an intricate life story and the characters were providing me with their back story. Each being woven into the Royal Oak's story and the story of others too. Oddly, as I would soon come to understand, one person's story may also include that of another person. This other person though was no longer with us, and most seem to be connected to the late 1800s, a period of time when the Royal Oak was owned by the Stevens family. That story would soon become as prominent to the haunting of the Royal Oak as the pub's locals that I had met and provided me with their many experiences whilst at the pub.

It seems odd that how the little pocket watch behaved would strangely provide some important information to keep in mind when thinking about the Royal Oak. The pocket watch was a connection to my past, to my grandfather, to family too. It was also an indication of time, but not time we observe in our day-to-day lives as time only seemed to run when it was needed. These elements would soon be reminders of the experiences, the connections and greater story that the Royal Oak would provide me with during my investigations.

Chapter Two

An Incipient Haunting

All stories tend to have a beginning; we open the cover of a book, thumb through the first few pages to find that first paragraph that introduces us to the story we are about to read. We have all experienced stories in various levels throughout our lives and those stories have helped to shape aspects of what makes us what we are today. Those stories have taught us that we will experience a beginning, a middle and an end; the paranormal does not like to follow those rules and the story I would find at the Royal Oak would certainly help me to redefine my understanding of this.

The initial interviews with some of the Royal Oak locals and the outcome of our first overnight investigation of the location began to plot a story that was far more complex than I realised straight away. It would be far more than a purported haunted location that we would investigate hoping to capture some paranormal activity, it would help me to learn much more about psychical research. However, it would have me question where the story of the Royal Oak truly began and where it may eventually end.

I had never heard of the Royal Oak in Swanage back in 2010 until my friend and fellow investigator Aaron brought it to my attention in March of that year. He had stumbled across a social media post where comments had been made regarding some paranormal activity experienced by the landlady, the staff and pub locals. As this seemed to indicate a mixture of physical activity and possible apparitional sightings, we saw it as a location that may provide us with a) an investigation that would be slightly different from what we were usually used to, and b) a location that was more like a private investigation location than the public ones we were used to. At that point in time, we did not really envisage that we or at least I would continue to return to the pub repeatably for the next twelve-plus years.

So, my beginning associated to the Royal Oak was in April, 2010, when Aaron and I visited Rachael for the first time to discuss what had been experienced there and gain an understanding of this potential case. A case which has continued to grow in various directions over the years and provided numerous experiences for those that have joined me on my trips to Swanage. In a way the location has also been a place where I have been able to carry out numerous experiments regarding the paranormal, but equally somewhere that I have learnt a great deal with regard to my own psychical research.

When I began to investigate the Royal Oak, my approach was focussed more on analysing the potential phenomena that I was presented with and then defining possible logical explanations for the most of it, reducing it to few if any actual points of activity which could be considered paranormal. I guess at that point in my life I was more focussed on relying on logic to explain away the oddities that I often encountered, but that was not to say that those oddities did not actually occur, more of a situation where if I could find a logical explanation then it was likely not something supernatural.

However, the Royal Oak would begin to change all that for me and certainly have me look at the bigger picture with that logical mind, but also with elements of philosophy and perhaps even the mind of a theorist working out ideas that could begin to help explain some of the phenomena I encountered. The key to this mindset change was really two things which were interconnected even though this was not really obvious from our original visit: 1) the people that I found at the Royal Oak were very much a part of the story here, their involvement and engagement as I investigated the case was imperative, and

2) the location itself and its history would be the stage that this story played out on across time. In the past and to an extent since, most investigations I have attended have been what I would call public events that occurred overnight with little interactions from locals. These ranged from visits to purported haunted locations with various Paranormal Events Groups to investigations I would organise for groups of friends within the field. That said though, even the latter was not much different from the format I found in the public events. The point being is that the Royal Oak case certainly began to take the shape of a private case from early in my visits. It is because of this that I am glad that I took notes in my journal from those first visits, right up until the last time I dropped into the pub in 2022 before starting to write this book.

Aaron and I made the trip to Swanage in early April, 2010, as far as can I remember as that is probably the least documented part of this story. We met with Rachael at the Royal Oak and if memory does serve me well, she provided us with a lovely lunch which we tucked into whilst beginning to discuss the high strangeness occurring at the pub. I have to admit, at that point in time I may well have been convinced that we could explain the activity logically and to an extent I think we could, but there were a few aspects that remained to stump us. This would become a common narrative for the Royal Oak, we would find a few paranormal occurrences that we could find explanations for, but each time we did we would equally find more that had no explanations or at least would begin to reside in what could only be described as a more spiritual aspect.

I am also pretty sure that following our pub lunch (with no alcohol by the way), Rachael took us on a tour of the pub. Interestingly, the pub appeared to have varying activity occurring throughout. Initially, I thought the activity may be focussed in some areas on the ground floor and perhaps one or two in other places around the building.

Whilst scribbling down some of the listed activity, I could feel my interest being truly peaked by the location, especially if it was all true and more importantly if we could experience some of it for ourselves. This was simply because the phenomena being described was something that could be potentially associated with a poltergeist type haunting and certainly with a hugely active location; something for me that was unheard of in the locations I had investigated, but present in the literature of the many books I spent my spare time reading. The reason I was leaning towards a poltergeist type case at that point was because the activity included phenomena ranging from physical object movement, footsteps, apparitional sightings, knockings or taps, odd feelings, strange smells and certainly other audible oddities. More on those in a little more detail later.

On the ground floor, activity seemed to be centred around the bar, the back room, the dining room, the door to the first floor and behind the bar. The first floor had activity centred around the main corridor and the bedroom with the loft space above it. Oddly at this point whilst Rachael did allude towards activity occurring in the other bedrooms and the kitchen on the first floor, we did not really focus much on these. Heading up one more flight of stairs to the second floor, activity was said to be focussed on the top bedroom with two single beds in it, later we would call this the twin room.

The location was certainly one that could be seen as providing great opportunities for paranormal investigators, with reported activity throughout the building and those reports being made by various sources, it seem a little too good to be true and I have to admit my sceptical side was already leading me to determine that perhaps we would find logical explanations for these experiences in good time. That said there was certainly an undeniable feel to the place, which remained just out of reach, hidden from view, that would connect with certain people and draw them in, making them a part of the story. Initially, I did not believe that would happen to me too, but as I look back over the years, it is completely obvious that I was connected and fascinated with the place from early on in my relationship with the pub.

After our tour of the Royal Oak and the many paranormal hotspots that seem to exist within its walls, Aaron and I met with a few of the locals that frequent the pub on a regular basis to gain their understanding of the high strangeness said to occur at their local. As expected, some had never experienced a thing while they popped in for a drink, but a few certainly advised that they had witnessed some weirdness at the Royal Oak during their visits. Some of these passing remarks did seem to relate to the experiences that Rachael had conveyed to us, like apparitional sightings, pictures falling off the wall and footsteps above the bar area when there was no one up there.

Our initial visit to the Royal Oak was a positive one, we had established a good understanding of the potential paranormal activity that was said to occur within the property. We had also established that these experiences had not only been something that the landlady had experienced, other visitors and staff had equally encountered them too. However, not everyone that visited the pub had experienced its potentially haunted side and the only spirits they had encountered were served in a glass. This was actually good news in my opinion, as if everyone we had spoken to had witnessed something paranormal then I would be inclined to question the statements and wonder more if they had been coached. The Royal Oak case was looking promising and I wanted to know more, explore the claims and see where we could find logical explanations. At that point, I was probably reasonably confident that I could explain away much of the activity, leaving only a few things to focus on. Aaron and I left the pub and headed home, already beginning to plan our return and an overnight investigation.

Following our initial visit to the Royal Oak in March, 2010, I wanted to return and perform a kind of reconnaissance; so, on Friday, 16 April, 2010, I drove back to Swanage to stay at the pub overnight. This would give me the opportunity to capture more information on the haunting and also begin to plan how my team would perform an investigation of the location.

After my arrival, I managed to catch up with Rachael around 21:20, at which point she advised me that some odd things had been occurring during the build-up to my arrival. This would become a commonality over the years, one which, at first, I thought was simply Rachael reading more into events than was required and then associating those with my pending arrival. However, the Royal Oak would begin to have a similar effect on me prior to my arrival. It would also begin to feel that as I passed through nearby Corfe Castle on my way to the Royal Oak, then through the winding lanes that pass through Harman's Cross and onto the outskirts of Swanage, previously known as Herston, I would very much feel as if I was on my way home. A strange feeling to have about a place that is over one hundred and fifty miles from your actual home. It was also a feeling that I never managed to really lose until the pandemic hit us all and my visits to Swanage stopped for a great deal of time.

Speaking to Rachael during that April, 2010, visit to Swanage, I quickly started to recognise that there was a great deal of spiritual input into the location from believers both resident to Swanage and also visiting on their holidays. The latter being relatively interesting, as it appeared that some people that were on their holidays in Swanage would for some reason be drawn to visit the pub. One such couple would become a part of our investigations later on during my time at the Royal Oak, more on them later.

Rachael also advised that she and some of her close friends held a spiritual circle at the Royal Oak, something which I did not know a great deal about at the time, but would certainly help to drive some of my own personal research, lead me to join the Society for Psychical Research (SPR) and also look into the Scole Experiment, which occurred in the 1990s and was investigated by members of the SPR. We often investigate locations with the assumption that with any luck we may find a few answers to the oddities that occur at the location, but as investigators we also know that often we leave with more questions; this was the first time that a location had prompted me to head down a completely different path.

This visit also brought to light something else which I had never encountered previously at other locations: the concept that there could be a connection between the living that were experiencing the paranormal at the pub and individuals that used to reside at the Royal Oak over one hundred years previously. Essentially, Rachael was suggesting the possibility, at this point, that both her and Andrew had entwined past lives that were related directly to the Royal Oak. Andrew was Rachael's friend, but as a dry stone waller he had originally come to the Royal Oak to repair the garden's dry stone wall. However, like me he had kept returning for various jobs. Like many, Andrew had a connection to the location and seemed oddly comfortable either side of the bar from my observation of his behaviour whilst at the pub. I think initially he was greatly cautious of my involvement, but equally curious. He was clearly well versed in philosophy too and an intelligent man; our conversations certainly indicated that when we had the time to converse.

Rachael highlighted that often she did not understand her own behaviour around Andrew, as she would become argumentative with him and on occasion that would escalate greatly. It was completely out of character and only happened in his presence. She was not herself and perhaps on occasions he was not himself either. Is it possible that when both were in the Royal Oak together their connection to their past lives was amplified to a point where they both became the past version of themselves? It was certainly something that I was not used to, but something I knew I had to explore. It was something that Rachael had begun to look into too and had a psychic medium friend who suggested that this could be the case.

The last thing that Rachael updated me on was the fact that she had recognised that many objects seem to continuously disappear: shoes, books and more. Often these objects would never reappear again, which is odd because if we misplace objects in our own home, they will often be discovered at a later date and we may then remember that we placed them at that location. In paranormal scenarios when objects tend to disappear but turn up again in locations we know we have already checked, this makes us question how they got there. The late Mary-Rose Barrington of the SPR called this "Just One of Those Things" or JOTT for short. It was certainly activity to take note of, as this was potentially the physical movement or removal of objects, which would not be an easy thing to achieve surely. It equally made me begin to believe that this may be some kind of poltergeist case, but it was certainly too early to draw conclusions.

I spoke with Andrew around 22:00 that same night, as with Rachael this was an informal chat. Andrew immediately indicated that he agreed with Rachael, and that there was certainly something occurring at the pub that required some investigation. I attempted to discuss Andrew's experiences at the pub, which at that point included seeing an apparition in the top bedroom, a vision of the ex-landlord in that same room and also picking up on a young girl being kept against her will in the pub.

We went on to discuss his fear of the pub due to these strange experiences and how he really did not like it there. This in turn sparked the question regarding why he seems to return so much and why the dry stone wall in the garden may have taken longer than expected, but Andrew simply indicated that this was the job and not related. A job which should have taken eight to ten weeks and went on beyond three months.

Oddly, Andrew asked if I was interested in hearing about the strange experiences he had when he was in his early twenties, which I was, of course. However, Andrew then stated that he was not ready to share such things.

He left me with little to go on at this point, but there certainly seemed to be some confusion around his reasons to continuously return to the Swanage pub. Perhaps, even though he indicated that he does not like the paranormal part of the pub or wish to know more, he is more interested than he lets on and really wishes to know more.

Around 23:00, I spoke with Rachael's friend Terri, who used to clean at the pub. However, as a medium, she used to regularly see spirits. Like Rachael and Andrew, Terri completely believes that there is something at the pub, convinced there is a greater story to be uncovered.

Given Terri's mediumship ability, I asked her to attempt to read me, which in all fairness she did really well, picking up on some personal unknown things. As this was also a reading she was not prepared for or realised it was going to occur until I asked, it provides greater value. It equally gave me additional confidence in Terri's ability as a medium. There was certainly an element of the spiritual side of things beginning to balance with the science approach.

Whilst I did sleep in one of the more purportedly haunted rooms, I did not really experience anything greatly paranormal. Although my phone's battery did drain down, which did surprise me; this was a new phone and as such I had to rule it out at the time as there was nothing to really connect it to, paranormally speaking.

Experiencing the pub for myself, interacting with the locals and capturing their stories was essential to my visit. Often as paranormal investigators, we find ourselves at public locations conducting an overnight investigation, but in reality, there has been limited activity in recent times. Over the space of say a decade there may have only been two or three reports of paranormal experiences; however, ghost hunters will still turn up with all their kit to find a ghost, often leaving after a quiet night. One way to try and understand the phenomena better is to capture witness statements and assess those to gain an understanding of how frequent paranormal events are in recent times, but also where at the location they occurred and at what time of day. There may be a pattern that can help with enabling investigators to focus their investigation.

The Royal Oak case was already beginning to shape up to be one that was more like a private residential case. As such, I gathered up a few experiences that the locals and staff may have had. This would help to understand the phenomena better and begin to design my own investigation.

I managed to find a few brief accounts of personal experiences at the Royal Oak, which I feel are important to include as they helped to shape our initial investigations. Interestingly, I felt these experiences were mostly apparitional visions, physical phenomena, audible phenomena and an odd display of mediumship.

In order to best provide the information related to the case, I have included these accounts below.

Experience One: "Sitting at the bar on our Chinese New Year, someone ran their finger right down my spine. I quickly turned around to see what Rachael wanted, only to find out she was not behind the bar and neither was anyone else, who did the finger belong to?"

Experience Two: "I was looking at Lauren, the barmaid, at the time she was heading for the wash-up-room. I was behind the bar. I watched her walk towards the fridge and turn the corner. The next minute she walked behind me! Who was that I saw walk over to the fridge then? Julie my friend at the bar saw my face and said, 'yes, I saw her too – who was that?'"

Experience Three: "One quiet afternoon last winter, there was only a handful in the pub. I was sat at the corner of the bar when I felt someone blow into my ear. I looked about; I was the only person at the bar. The nearest person to me was at least ten feet away." This experiencer goes on to say, "As we discussed what I had experienced, I glanced through to the stairs, the net curtain fell back into place, just as if someone had been looking out. Really feeling peculiar now, within two minutes the curtain moved again. Not like being blown by a draught, but as if someone picked it up and quickly dropped it again."

Experience Four: "A couple of Sundays ago, I was in the kitchen preparing Sunday roast, chopping vegetables on the top of the freezer, and I felt someone tug on the bottom of my T-Shirt." The experiencer then continued with, "Within two minutes my T-Shirt was tugged again." This same experiencer also spoke of various oddities that happened at the pub, mentioning odd bumps and bangs, doors creaking and the sound of old-fashioned door latches, of which there were none in the pub.

Experience Five: "In the beginning, I was hearing footsteps and the occasional bang from the rooms above (the bar, first floor)." This experiencer continues, "If I was looking for some 'proof' in ghostly goings-on, it came on Mother's Day this year (2009). A warm Sunday lunchtime I was working behind the bar and behind me was the door to upstairs. As I looked round, the net curtain covering the window fell – just like someone was 'peeping out' then dropped it. Not quite believing my eyes, I looked again and clearly saw it happen a second time."

Experience Six: "I had a very icy breath blow on my neck and at the same time my phone screen went completely blank."

Experience Seven: "By the chiller door, an area of the pub I probably could describe as my least favourite, I could smell hay, and when I closed my eyes, it clearly smelt of a damp stable. Unknown to me that area of the pub was previously used as stables, and somebody else had previously smelt the same thing!"

Experience Eight: "I decided to go into the other room where I was being involved in a meeting with the brewery. About ten minutes later a picture fell off the wall and hit the area manager on the arm, I didn't realise that at the time the area manager tried to hang the picture on the wall, I was later told by Ray that there was no picture hook on the wall neither a hole in the wall where it should have been, where did the picture come from? I was glad to leave the pub on that occasion, not realising what had just happened to me."

Experience Nine: "One cold winter's night I came into the bar and thought it would be lovely to take the nice big black tub chairs and put them by the roaring fire at the other end of the room. I placed the first chair by the fire and went back to move the second chair next to it, all fine I thought! I turned round to sit in the chair and as I did so I apologised to the lady that was sat in the chair whom I had nearly sat on. On looking again, she was not there!"

These experiences are taken not only from online accounts I have read, but in some cases I have also spoken to the individuals to hear their stories again. A few of the experiences are from the same people, but I have split them up as they occurred at different times.

I think these experiences outline the phenomena as it was originally understood to be. This included object movement, physical touch and apparitional encounters. There were also audible phenomena too, but this was fewer now.

Reviewing these statements again over twelve years later provided me with a different perspective than the one I had back in 2010. Originally, I was highly sceptical, seeking potential logical explanations or even questioning the individuals as I considered potential for fraud. Were all these pub locals so invested in their local pub that they were willing to lie about their paranormal claims?

Whilst as paranormal investigators we must always consider the potential for fraud, we must also consider that someone may truly believe they have had an experience, which they can only define as being paranormal. That is, they are unable to find any other explanation at the time. Often when it comes to the paranormal, there are two main drivers for fraud in my opinion; these are financial gain or some kind of attention, which is often mistaken for fame. I have certainly read about cases such as these where one or both drivers come into play. For me a classic example is the 30 East Drive, Pontefract, or the Black Monk of Pontefract Case. Whilst the original two instances of potential poltergeist activity are not in dispute here, I rather question the location's current use as a place that paranormal groups must investigate. Another "most haunted location" that people rave about. However, the reality is that the location that is dressed up like the set of the movie *When the Lights Went Out* (2012), which tells the story of those paranormal events, actually makes a great deal of money from ghost hunters willing to pay for a night in the haunted 30 East Drive.

The point here being that whilst 30 East Drive may be truly haunted as there is certainly plenty documented on the events in the 1960s, the location is being very cleverly marketed at the time of writing this book as a hotspot of activity. As such one must question the true intent behind setting up this historic haunted hotspot and charging quite high prices for ghost hunting groups to spend the night in a pretty standard residential home. In regard to this specific location, I have discussed with many paranormal investigators and ghost hunters, and to be honest they are pretty divided. Some believe it to be a fraud, scamming people out of their money, whilst others claim to have had remarkable experiences at the location. So, how can we really understand which it may be? That really depends on the individual, I suppose; initially, I was convinced the location was a fraud, as our understanding of poltergeist cases meant they would last for a few months and then stop. However, the original case broke that rule by returning a couple of years later. Is it possible that the presence of some ghost hunters actually draws out that activity? I could not rule it out for 30 East Drive, and I would not be able to rule it out for the Royal Oak either.

Whilst the owners of 30 East Drive happily ensured many ghost hunters would part with their hard-earned cash, and ensured their location became very famous amongst ghost hunters, Rachael at the Royal Oak just seemed to want us to help her to understand the odd occurrences over the years. In fact, in all the time I have known her she has never charged me to run an investigation at the Royal Oak. In fact, I had to convince her to charge others a little for ghost hunt events or similar, simply because I knew she was closing up early and losing out on potential earnings. Even then what she did charge was way under the market rate. This always convinced me that even though like many pubs across the country, the Royal Oak was struggling to keep afloat, Rachael wanted to understand the phenomena occurring in her pub, rather than exploit it or even expel it. Whilst at times it could be scary, it was a part of the pub itself, its history and it had a story it wanted to share with us.

So, whilst as an investigator I always consider the possibility of fraud in any paranormal case, I also take time to understand the story being told to me. A story, in this case, which was conveyed by Rachael and the locals, but also, little by little, by the building itself. The immediate history and more distant, too, was willing to share a little here and there, revealing a part of the mystery but never quite enough.

It was always important for me to discuss the Royal Oak with its former landlady and her family. Sharan equally has a story to tell, therefore it was enough for me to understand that the Royal Oak had been experiencing the paranormal long before Rachael took over as landlady.

In fact, when I interviewed Sharan, albeit briefly during those initial visits to the Royal Oak, I was half expecting to hear that she had been at the pub months prior to Rachael. However, I was a little thrown off course when she told me that she used to be the landlady but had left nearly ten years ago.

Until this point the paranormal experiences, as far as I knew, only reached back to around 2009. Now we had a timeline that potentially reached back another ten years to around 2000. At the point of writing this book, we had a possible twenty-two plus years of paranormal activity. This also meant that at this point in the investigation, Sharan's experiences became our "paranormal alpha report". A term I picked up from Detective Greg Lawson's book, *Detecting Paranormal*. In fairness it's a common process used by paranormal investigators to determine the timeline of the events and experiences encountered at a location. Often understanding the "paranormal alpha report" can help us to understand how a case may have evolved.

On this occasion I was not only fortunate to talk to the person who was the first person to possibly experience high strangeness at the Royal Oak, but she provided us with a tour of where she had these experiences.

We began our tour on the second floor in the twin bedroom. Sharan advised us that she would see a man looking up at the window from the corner of the garden; what was odd was that she would not see the roofs of the houses, instead there would be an orchard behind the man. It is believed that beyond the pub garden wall where there is now a housing estate there was once an orchard. However, I was unable to confirm this, but still it would have been countryside leading to the nearby quarries.

Moving to the landing outside the twin bedroom, Sharan told us how the family cat was seriously spooked by something. So much so it was visibly scared and had its claws out ready to attack, but there was nothing to be seen. The cat, as far as Sharan was aware, never returned to the second floor.

Ducking our heads and heading down the stairs to the first-floor landing, Sharan shared with us how her children would hear footsteps on the landing most nights. As any investigators know and probably most parents with young children, heating pipework can often sound like footsteps as they warm up or cool down. However, Sharan assured me these were heavy and distinct footsteps. Possibly more like someone wearing boots.

In the far room off what was then a sitting room, Sharan mentioned something about finding stairs to the kitchen in the corner behind a studded wall. Also, they discovered a hidden loft room above this room. Sharan advised that the room always felt odd and it never felt welcoming to them, so they never used it. She informed us that they were told that someone was kept in the room against their will but would not elaborate on this. It was an odd space, but at that point in time it simply felt unused to me.

Whilst Sharan's partner, Kev, was in the roof space, he had something touch the back of his neck several times. Of course, thinking logically, as a roof space, it's likely Kev encountered spiders' webs or similar. However, I cannot simply rule this experience out; just because there is a possible logical explanation does not mean that is the actual explanation.

Interestingly, Sharan told us about the curtain at the bottom of the stairs moving in a similar way. She also told us of pictures being thrown from walls in the back room on the ground floor and some physical activity in the main bar.

At one point they found what was identified as a human vertebra bone in the garden, whilst digging a hole. After finding this, Sharan saw an apparition of a man. The bone was said to be dated over three hundred years old and as such too old to investigate by local police. Following this discovery, tapping on people's necks became a regular occurrence.

Following our tour of the Royal Oak with former landlady Sharan, she provided her theory. She believed a woman was murdered by the man whose apparition she saw as seeing him presented Sharan with immense fear. She believed this may have happened over three hundred years ago. She also believes there is a relationship to the top twin bedroom with this and the bone they discovered. Sharan went on to advise that she saw in her mind a middle-aged woman dressed up every Sunday in her Sunday best. This was possibly an ex-landlady; she asked a local who confirmed her description at the time. She was described as wearing a light blue two-piece outfit. For some reason unknown to Sharan she would sometimes wear some nice pearls, hence the Sunday best theory. It was an interesting theory, but one which would be hard to clarify.

Sharan's account certainly changed my understanding of the Royal Oak case, especially as we were now looking at a timeline that reached back considerably further than a few months or years. We were only at the beginning of our investigation and already a decade late.

However, perhaps the Royal Oak's current landlady has what could be seen as a somewhat interesting path to her place behind the bar of this purported haunted establishment.

Rachael originally took on the Royal Oak as its landlady in May, 2006, but this was far from her first encounter with the pub. She believes that her very first visit to the Royal Oak may have been as far back as the 1980s when she popped in for a drink. At this point it was nothing more than a local pub; there was nothing special or memorable about her visit.

That said and come 1985 to 1990, Rachael found herself behind the bar at the Royal Oak for the first time. She took a job working there. She also recalls that at one point she was sent upstairs for something and finding herself alone on the first floor, she realised she did not like it. When I asked Rachael about this experience, she could not provide any real additional information other than that the younger version of herself just did not like the feeling she had upstairs at the Royal Oak. Whilst I would like to take this experience and state that it should be seen as the new "paranormal alpha report", it was never logged as a paranormal experience. It is simply a feeling alone and most importantly, this information only came to light following questioning from me. As such it was not a truly memorable encounter that would cause Rachael to mention it earlier. This does not mean it did not occur, just its significance was not seen to be great enough until a line of questioning brought it to the surface.

However, I will remain open minded that the activity at the Royal Oak may possibly have been present as far back as the 1980s. That would mean that we could be looking at over forty years of haunting, maybe more.

Whilst working at the Royal Oak between 1985 and 1990, Rachael never returned upstairs alone. Shortly after, she left to work in a different pub. Although it makes for a good story, Rachael said that she could not say if she left due to her experience or if she simply got a better offer at another pub. Either way, she moved on putting the Royal Oak behind her or so she thought.

Around fifteen years later Rachael applied for the post of landlady at a nearby pub called the Globe; however, the Royal Oak would find its way back into Rachael's life.

In 2005, as Rachael walked with her friend Terri, she was advised that she would have the Royal Oak. This was information provided by Terri psychically. Whilst Rachael would not usually question her friend's ability, on this occasion she did so with good reason. Rachael had already signed all the paperwork to become the landlady at the Globe, so it was a done deal in her mind. Equally, Rachael wanted nothing to do with the Royal Oak at that point in time. To her it was something that Terri must have got completely wrong. Rachael did also advise that her grandfather, at some point, made the same claim that she would run the Royal Oak. However, at that time it just did not seem remotely possible, let alone likely.

However, soon after the Globe fell through, and Rachael lost out on becoming its landlady. Then in May, 2006, she was offered the Royal Oak, just as Terri had predicted. I think Rachael finally accepted the Royal Oak in May, 2006, after refusing it a few times first. However, even though she was the landlady, Rachael initially did not live in the pub. This would come later when a major operation, which made walking and driving very difficult, forced her to take up residence there. It was on that first weekend living at the pub that her friends from Norfolk, who had come to help, saw an apparition of a woman that they thought was Rachael. Perhaps that's where her paranormal encounters at the pub truly began?

Nearly four years later, after Rachael and I had met for the first time, she was given the opportunity to purchase the Royal Oak from the brewery and make the pub completely hers. Whilst this was no simple task for Rachael, it was one that presented itself around her fiftieth birthday in December, 2010. Perhaps it was a gift she could not pass up and after much deliberation, she moved forward with the purchase of the Royal Oak in early 2011.

So, as I began my time investigating the oddities that were being experienced at the Royal Oak, it changed hands from being brewery owned to become Rachael's very own pub. A venture that these days is by no means an easy one, especially for publicans in more rural areas such as Swanage. Whilst I very much respect Rachael's decision to become her own boss, as an investigator of the paranormal I had to be mindful of the situation. Especially as I knew that claims of paranormal activity can often be used to bring in various ghost hunting groups and generate income. However, in all my time visiting and investigating the Royal Oak, Rachael has never charged me. I know that over the years she has charged a few teams and events teams as she was losing income from normal trade. Rachael still never charged anyone too much and, in my opinion, probably still made a loss on the Ghost Hunts. The point being that hosting Ghost Hunts and charging groups was not something I considered to be a reason for potential fraud. In fact, it is my belief that Rachael genuinely wants to know more about the paranormal activity occurring within the walls of the Royal Oak.

From listening to Rachael's prior experiences at the Royal Oak, the experiences of the pub's locals, and an experience of a previous landlady, I was beginning to understand that there was something potentially going on there and I knew that something at the Royal Oak was becoming apparent. Whatever was happening at this quiet pub near to the UK's south coast, was certainly going to keep me searching for answers and learning so much more about psychical research.

This investigation was going to be all about stories: Rachael's story; the pub's history; anyone that could stumble upon the Royal Oak and find themselves having an odd experience there; those brought there by stories of ghosts and, of course, those times when some of the stories appear to cross-over or blend with one another. Like any good story, the one of the Royal Oak comes with its fair share of complexities, but also moments I will take with me into the rest of my life.

Much of this would become apparent as I returned to the Royal Oak once again to investigate. I would be introduced to more of the pub's past and potentially visions of my own.

Chapter Three

Strange Connections

Often investigations of purported haunted locations for me do not simply begin when we arrive; there is usually some planning involved and before that some thinking. The thinking part is something that I have always done my best to document in the many journals I have kept over the years. Anyone that has been on an investigation with me would have at some point seen me scribbling into a journal, making notes on any oddities that may be occurring. These notes have often turned into blog posts on my website (ashleyknibb.com).

However, those notes taken in between, the documenting of my thoughts, has mostly remained within the pages of my journals out of public view. So, perhaps as a part of bringing you more about the Royal Oak, I could share some of those thoughts. In all fairness, I do not think I have much choice. Especially as many of those thoughts were directly related to the Royal Oak case. I have come to recognise that many paranormal cases do not remain at one location. Something which may indicate the source of these hauntings may be more related to their common denominator, which would be us, the living.

In the time before I would return to the Royal Oak to attempt a second investigation, I was staying at my parents' home in Wales with my children. During my time there I had some time to review some research from previous investigations, which included a visit to Bradwell Abbey in Milton Keynes and various research I had been reading up on. At that time this provided me with a potential sequence of events, which seemed to occur at the time when more notable phenomena were happening. Whilst it was not an exact science, it certainly sparked my interest enough to make a note of its presence.

The high strangeness of this sequence of events meant that the phenomena were not always uniform in their appearance. Something which I know science would not be particularly pleased about, as for something to be repeatable we want the pattern to be the same each time. This observation would not conform in this manner though. Sometimes only a few of the events would occur, and sometimes they would occur at speed, and sometimes they would be so slow in their occurrence that they could be missed. However, the more of these that occurred, the more likely the phenomena would be witnessed. In some cases, like an investigation at Peterborough Museum, using music from the 1916s did seem to speed up the process, but, of course, we cannot be one hundred per cent sure of this.

These strange notable events, in no particular order, are as follows.

1. The Darkening – This is where the light in a room (or area) seems to seep out, so that it appears darker than it was previously witnessed to be. Something that can occur quickly, where you suddenly recognise a room to be darker than it previously was, or slowly, when you witness a room get darker as you stand within it. As paranormal investigators or ghost hunters often work in the dark this may seem obvious, but I have on many occasions heard investigators utter the words "has it just got darker in here, or is it me?" Then more of the group notice.
2. The Temperature Drop – This is something now classically associated with ghost hunting, often more know as "cold spots". Again, this can happen quickly or slowly. Generally, this is picked up by an individual feeling colder but also identified as "cold spots" within a space. Much like the light, the heat is drained from a room (area). However, this is not just something that may

occur to a room or area of a building as I have witnessed an individual appear to have the heat drained from them, so they are icy to the touch.

3. The Moving Shadows – Following the room darkening, sometimes shadows or at least something moving about is witnessed. Often this is only noted through peripheral vision, but I know of instances where something has moved and blocked out the light for which there was no explanation at the time.
4. The Audible Phenomena – Often some kind of audible phenomena is heard, which may range from taps to actual voices speaking.
5. The Visual Phenomena – Similar to the shadows, strange things can start to be observed. This can often be as simple as odd moving lights, right up to apparitions.
6. The Feeling of Change – The investigator may also become aware of a change about them. This could be described as a change in the atmosphere, or a feeling that something is heavier or uncomfortable. It is difficult to describe on paper, but during an investigation you are just aware that something is no longer as it was previously.

These six points are simply a rough guide, as they may appear in any order, may not all occur, but when they do, I have witnessed more phenomena occur. Observations worth keeping an eye out for perhaps. However, these are just that, observations I have made, and not proven facts of the paranormal. There is a lack of data to support them in that way at present.

In 2013, I was less read than I am today and whilst I still agree that the presence of these six events could mean increased activity, I am not sure I totally agree with my 2013 theories of this being related to energy specifically and I feel that spiritual energy is a stretch I am unable to make. However, there is a common denominator in all these events: us, the investigator or experiencer. Understanding this was something that began to show me other potential explanations for paranormal activity.

Ahead of my June, 2013, investigation at the Royal Oak, it would seem I was contemplating these kinds of things and more according to my journal. On 1 June, 2013, I outlined how I knew this upcoming investigation would be more spiritually led, but even then I was unsure how that would be planned. However, on this occasion I would be heading down a few days before the investigation to gain a better understanding for the pub and some of the locals.

On Thursday, 6 June, 2013, at around seven thirty in the evening, I arrived back in Swanage. The Royal Oak was reasonably quiet but sitting at the bar were the familiar faces of Rachael and Andrew.

It was odd returning to the Royal Oak again and this time for an in-depth investigation. It also felt like home oddly or at least like a place that was a part of my life, not just another investigation location. In all my years investigating, no other location has felt like this, it made me wonder what kind of impact this place was having on me. I guess then I never considered that ten years later I would be writing about a decade-plus of visits and investigations at the little Swanage pub.

I took a little time to acclimatise myself with the place and then slowly began to talk with a few people. Sometimes in these situations and especially at the Royal Oak, I have found that during simple conversation many will volunteer their stories. What is also nice is that within that setting people provide more than just a ghost story, they give a little more about themselves too. In that you learn about their experiences and not just another ghost story.

Rachael had plenty to tell me about the latest at the pub and even Andrew told me that on this occasion I would certainly find something. At that point I probably politely received his comment unaware of what was coming. Although he could just have been really lucky with his comments, or even influenced me somehow. More on that later.

After Andrew left, Rachael, Luka, one of the pub's latest residents, and I headed for dinner at a local Indian restaurant just down the road. During a lovely curry and a pint of Cobra lager, Luka advised that it was important to know that before his own experience at the Royal Oak he was completely sceptical and did not believe in the haunting.

However, what I found odd about this experience was something I would hear quite often during my time at the Royal Oak. Apparently, Rachael would almost guide people to do certain things or go somewhere in the pub and the result would be an experience of some kind.

On this occasion, Rachael had told Luka to check upstairs. He did, expecting to see nothing as usual, but actually saw a girl asking him to play or follow her, which he did all the way to Rachael's room, where she vanished. Rachael said he came downstairs looking shocked, but described the girl's dress with such detail it was evident that something odd had occurred.

Later on that evening I would also speak to Mo, whose abilities could be best described as trance mediumship. Mo shared with me numerous accounts where he had encountered spirits at the Royal Oak. Some of which he believed he had seen as apparitions. Incidentally one such apparition was a young girl, perhaps the very same one experienced by Luka.

One regular at the pub also shared a video that had been captured on a mobile phone, which showed a woman in the pub engaged in automatic writing. At least that is what I was told at the time and took it at face value. Watching the video, it looked very much like a teacher marking work rather than someone writing something specific. It was not the best video and unfortunately what was written was unavailable, which means the most important information was missing on this occasion.

Although I had arrived the previous evening, it was really the morning of Friday, 7 June, 2013, that truly felt like the investigation had begun.

As I entered the now empty bar area, I found Martin cleaning the pub. Without so much as a coffee to help me wake up at that point, I took the opportunity to ask Martin some questions. I was half expecting him to tell me that he had never had any experiences, but that was not to be the case. In fact, Martin was more than happy to share many of his experiences.

Like many at the pub he had seen a few apparitions at various places around the place. He mentioned a woman in white as being one such experience. Oddly he also mentioned a drawing that was on the wall near the bar; according to Martin it would change its expression from time to time. On that particular day the woman in the drawing was smiling, I hoped that was a good thing.

As we continued to talk, Martin recalled a strange event when he believed a piece of horse dung appeared out of thin air. I asked if he touched or picked it up, and he said he picked it up to simply clarify what it was. He was unable to determine if it was hot or cold to the touch, something I asked. I also asked why he thought that of all the possible objects to appear out of nowhere, a piece of horse dung would be something that did. He did not really know but could only advise what he had found.

Before continuing it is probably worth evaluating this single event briefly. What Martin has described is commonly known as an apport or a materialised object. This kind of activity is often associated to poltergeist cases such as the Enfield Poltergeist Case described by Guy Lyon Playfair in his book *This House Is Haunted* or cases that include large amounts of physical phenomena such as the Scole Experiment described in the Society for Psychical Research's Scope Report. Whilst physical phenomena had been mentioned and potentially experienced up to this point, I was not aware of apports being reported.

Later Rachael would also share events where potentially but not categorically conclusive, objects would also simply disappear.

Martin's experience could really only have one probable and reasonable explanation: that the encountered horse dung was dropped by Rachael's father who tended the Royal Oak's garden. He may have been using it to help fertilise the flowers. As such, Martin may have been unaware that he had passed through the pub at the time, discovering the item in question and knowing of the pub's stories of the paranormal, plus his own apparitional experiences; he concluded that it was paranormal.

However, although this explanation can seem relatively robust, there are problems. We are not able to determine if on this occasion Rachael's father was in the garden or even used horse dung on the garden. That piece of information eludes us. It's a possibility, but not something we can prove in relation to that specific event.

The paranormal possibility is that this particular apport relates to the blacksmith's premises that is said to have been situated at the Royal Oak in its past. Again, not evidential, but a possibility connected to the beliefs of those at the pub.

Suffice to say, this is an event experienced only by Martin that will remain personal to him and something that is certainly difficult to prove. That said, I do not believe there is a reason to say that this event did not take place. Martin provided an event which was not one you would likely make up as it has no meaning. It is simply something that occurred and something that Martin had no understanding of, nor could he provide an explanation as to why it occurred. It was as it was, just one of those things I suppose.

Once he had finished cleaning the pub, a little less interrupted by this psychical researcher, Martin headed off. I began to realise that the pub could often be this way; from time to time you would bump into the odd local and before you knew it, you would be engaged in their story of paranormal experiences at the Royal Oak. Although equally there were also those locals that had frequented the pub for many years and were still yet to have their own experience to talk about. Still, I guess that these things do not happen to us all.

A short while later, Terri, Rachael's friend and a medium, arrived at the pub to talk to me. This encounter would turn out to be a little on the odd side as it was not so much about her or the Royal Oak, but more about me. This was strange as I often seem to be quite closed off to mediums.

Terri immediately picked up on the fact that I had changed slightly, especially when it came to aspects more associated with spirituality. Whilst I could not be considered a total believer, all of a sudden I had certainly become more interested in the possibility that belief in spirituality added to the phenomena I was investigating. In other investigations and in much of the material I was reading, belief was a huge factor and as such I knew it could not be discounted from the equation of such phenomena. At that point in my own journey into a wider understanding of the paranormal, I was certainly moving away from a simpler comprehension of the phenomena and realising it was far more complex and interlinked than I had previously thought. It was beyond a location being haunted, it was more about us, about consciousness and perhaps how connected we all may be. It's possible that this new viewpoint was not something hidden inside my mind alone. Perhaps I was outwardly displaying this new understanding by the things I did and what I said. Even so, Terri saw that change and called it out.

As we began to talk, Terri mentioned that my grandfather, Len, was standing over me. Whilst this may have been seen to many as an easy way to gain my trust, and as such may see it as being untrue, I decided to embrace the statement and really just go with it. So, I passed Terri my grandfather's pocket watch to hold.

What happened next was interesting and given that Terri was holding his pocket watch, could be regarded as psychometry. Of course, psychometry is believed to be the ability to know information about events or a person just by touching an object that may have been associated with them. To be honest, I do not believe that I had encountered anyone having success in this area, let alone the information provided by Terri on this occasion.

Terri began by picking up on several names directly related to my family. These were Alice, Arthur, Alan, Chris, Albert and Francis. Whilst I knew and could place the first four straight away, Albert and Francis escaped me. However, following a catch-up with my mother, it quickly became apparent that the names Albert and Francis were also related to my grandfather's family. In fact, his wife Edith's brother was called Albert. Whilst my mother knew of Francis being connected to her mother, the family records did not make it clear whether or not Francis was male or female.

However, this was not all the information that Terri provided. She also advised that she picked up on the name Milligan. Now for years I believed that my grandfather was Spike Milligan's gardener at one point, a belief I had obviously come to through misremembering the true facts, which I may have overheard as a younger version of myself. My grandfather was the gardener for the house next door to Spike Milligan's house. This does begin to raise some questions around the source of the information and whether the source of that information is my grandfather's spirit or my own mind.

Continuing, Terri also mentioned elephants being relevant to my grandfather, which could be related to his tour in Burma during WWII. She also mentioned steam trains but admitted that she was hesitant regarding this as she knew Swanage has a steam railway. However, she did say that he could tell you a great deal about steam trains, which was completely true.

He was a model railway enthusiast and had an impressive model railway that entertained my siblings, my cousins and I for hours when we were younger. Oddly, Terri also mentioned that there was rhubarb which grew in my grandfather's garden. Rhubarb was something he enjoyed, but also my mother used to pinch it and eat it raw.

The session ended with Terri convincing me to head into town for a little while, which I did. On the way I got a little lost and stumbled on the steam engines' shed with an amazing turn table. That reminded me of the shed in my grandfather's garden that contained his model steam engines and a similar turn table. There was also a fabulous green (a colour mentioned by Terri) locomotive (4-6-2) and some Pullman coaches in the nearby station. In that moment I felt close to my grandfather; the memories of taking various trips on steam trains around the country flooded back. More importantly, though, I remembered the time spent in his beautiful garden watching the model trains, something I had almost lost since his death. I was reminded of the importance of family, of how lucky I was to have the upbringing I did, how close and supportive we are too. I was also reminded of another positive of mediumship I had not thought of: the comfort it can bring when you have lost a loved one.

When I returned to the Royal Oak following my brief exploration of Swanage, there was another lady working the bar whose name, I think, was Katie. I took the opportunity to ask her if she had experienced anything odd at the pub and was surprised to hear her tell me about an apparitional encounter with a woman in white. I began to wonder if this could be the woman called Bernadette, whom Andrew had picked up on during his original visit. Whilst it was interesting that a woman in white kept being mentioned, it was not uncommon for a purported haunted location to have reports of a woman in white. In fact, sightings of women in white as ghosts are reasonably common, which immediately lends the conversation of our haunting source to become one of potential survival or perhaps something more in relation to the human mind. A relationship which could be associated with psi abilities. Is it spirit or is it our mind which is giving power to this phenomenon? We shall tackle these questions in greater detail later.

At this point, I headed upstairs to my room to do a little research and preparation for the investigation the following night. What was strangely odd about the Royal Oak was how comfortable I felt whilst I was there, it just felt like home. It was like I belonged and although I was essentially an outsider investigating their paranormal claims, I felt like one of the locals. Something I would have to be very mindful of to ensure that it did not present a bias in my investigation.

Whilst upstairs I took some time to scribble down a bit of a plan, and as we were attempting a seance, I wondered if it could be influenced by making a note of some names to keep in mind. In review of this list now and knowing more of the subject, I can see that I tried to provide too many names.

My list read as follows.

- Harry Houdini (illusionist)
- Harry Price (investigator)
- Helen Duncan (medium)
- Arthur Conan Doyle (author)
- T S Elliot (author)
- Margaret, Kate & Leah Fox (mediums)
- Thomas Edison (inventor)
- Montague Keen (SPR investigator of Scoles Experiment)
- Arthur Ellison (SPR investigator of Scoles Experiment)
- David Fontana (SPR investigator of Scoles Experiment)
- Paschal Beverly Randolph (trance medium)
- Emma Hardinge Britten (trance medium)

- Leonora Piper (trance medium)
- Len Larbey (my grandfather, mother's side)
- William Herbert Knibb (my grandfather, father's side)
- Walter Ronald (connected to Mat – team member)
- Derek Butler (connected to Mat – team member)
- Catherine Gullivan (connected to Mat – team member)

Similar to the Scoles Experiment, I hoped all or at least some may get involved. I was hoping perhaps for my own spirit team. Again, as I review this list now, I see that it's not only too long, but extremely ambitious. What I should have done was either picked one or two names, or simply saw who came through by themselves. However, my aims were pretty straight forward in relation to a classical seance. I was hoping for mental mediumship, trance mediumship and if we were really lucky, potentially physical mediumship. I certainly had heard of mental and trance mediumship taking place at the Royal Oak, but physical mediumship was only theoretical based on various reports. I also hoped that focussing on these would provide us with direct voice, a kind of channelling, apports; audible phenomena; physical phenomena and visual phenomena. Again, in review of my desired outcome, I feel I may have been somewhat ambitious. One thing that I did feel was important was for the group to conduct a walk around of various rooms prior to the seance to allow us to bond as a group.

As a part of my efforts to plan ahead, I made a drawing of the seance table that we would set up during the evening. Knowing those that would attend I then proceeded to write their names in particular positions around the table, ensuring that there was also an empty chair. This would mean that there would be thirteen chairs around the table, with twelve people attending. At the time I made a note in my journal stating that I believed some people should not be present and that the numbers may reduce to nine; the reason for this I do not know.

After spending a little time upstairs, I decided to head downstairs to the bar area to observe the locals during a regular evening at the Royal Oak which was on this occasion a Karaoke Night. In all honesty the place was similar to any local pub that one may encounter on a Friday night. My only real observation was that it was more like a family home during some kind of party. Unsurprisingly, Rachael fitted into this environment perfectly, similar to a well-respected family member or even perhaps the head of the family. I remember thinking that this is exactly what many local pubs probably lack these days, a sense of community that brings people together like a family.

The bustle of the pub was certainly intoxicating, with various ages grouped about the bar, the back Pool Room and also in the garden. There were the regulars, which I recognised now, most of which were older and sat either at the bar or around the fireplace. Then there were the few that seemed to interact with those regulars but maintained a seat elsewhere in the bar. Then in the Pool Room were a few younger visitors to the pub that I had not seen before, passing through on their way down to the town centre for their Friday night out. The garden seemed to bring together those from all groups and ages, through their common habit of smoking. Not one of my favourites, but oddly smoking does often bring those together in conversation who may not regularly do so. Perhaps in the case of the Royal Oak, this may also be a time and location where various stories of ghostly encounters may have been shared. Although that said, one subject that certainly did not appear to be taboo on the pub's premises was that of the paranormal. As such, I could not imagine anyone reserving themselves from discussing an experience should they have had one.

As I stood close to the bar, listening to the first brave locals step up to sing their chosen song, Mo walked in and it was not long before we started talking. Mo, or Michael, is quiet, softly spoken and down to earth as an individual. He was certainly not what I was expecting with regard to the individual that would later provide some very interesting trance mediumship sessions. However, I liked Mo a lot and have a great deal of time for him. I found him to be completely believable when speaking about his experiences and his mediumship. Often when discussing aspects of the paranormal with potential witnesses, I have found that many will misremember events and often will recount events that were actually the experiences of others. Whilst there is, in these circumstances, the possibility of fraud, often individuals just appear to be misremembering the events as their own. During our conversation Mo did not seem to do this, but quite the opposite, highlighting that some of what he had recounted was only known to him due to others advising him of said events after they occurred, when he was no longer in trance. This aligned with some of what I had read on the subject of mediumship, which suggested to me that we could be dealing with a genuine instance of trance mediumship.

Around 21:00 my younger sister, Leanne, arrived with her friend Mat at the Royal Oak. These were to join the investigation as a part of my team to primarily document the investigation on film. The pair were well versed in film and television process, as that is their day job and field of expertise. I have always wanted to make a documentary, but I'm just not sure of my creative capability within the area of film; I have kept myself to writing about the subject instead. Hopefully, that is where my own talents lay, they certainly have helped so far.

It was certainly good to see familiar faces at that point, but I already felt quite at home at the Royal Oak. Although, there was a part of me that was beginning to worry about that feeling, as I did not wish my personal connection to the pub to build a bias that may impact my investigation.

After Leanne, Mat and I popped upstairs to drop their stuff in my room, we returned to the bar and as we did so Rachael asked us to talk to Roy about his story. Whilst I was fully prepared to talk to potential witnesses of oddities at the pub, I have to admit that I thought I was finished for the day after speaking to Mo. I guess it just shows that when you immerse yourself in a case such as this, you are never really off-duty as you have to continue to capture information, witness statements and more all the time, in order to gain some kind of insight into what is going on.

Roy told us how one evening he was telling people information about themselves that he could not have known. My first thought was that he was potentially picking up information telepathically, which was interesting, especially as he was not associating this to his own possible ability, but more the pub itself was an influence on him. Rachael asked Roy to do the same for her, clearly curious to see how well he may do, but in that moment, he refused only to come back to her challenge later in the evening just before he would leave. However, his message to Rachael was simply "Bernadette".

Whilst a simple name on its own may seem like very little information to pass onto someone, and distinctly lacking in detail, for Rachael this was something that meant a great deal. At that point in our investigation, Rachael would associate the name Bernadette with herself, a probable spirit within the pub and also with Andrew.

Roy continued with his story; he told me that when he got home, he sat on the toilet and closed his eyes momentarily, but when he opened them he found himself outside the pub looking up at it. He shut his eyes and when he opened them again, he was back home. However, Roy's odd experiences did not end there as he would dream about the pub shortly after this event. He dreamt he was outside the cellar area, but there was a double door. In his dream, Roy witnessed an old man's head and body come through the doors. It then quickly disappeared. The experience clearly shook him a great deal. Roy then went on to identify this old man as the one with a beard in the large photograph near to the gentlemen's toilets. He also indicated that he had a little trouble looking at the photograph.

Interestingly, Roy then stated something different from what usually occurs when people tell me about their odd experiences: rather than wanting to know more about what was going on, he told me he wanted it fixed. He went on to express that he had never asked for this at all and did not want it. It was a strange one for me, as he was clearly curious to know more about what was going on with him and the strange activities at the pub, but in direct contrast to this he simply wanted it fixed and gone.

Now it may be important to add at this point that Roy was not someone that you may associate stereotypically with this sort of event or experience. He was a man that had a somewhat colourful past, let's say, and would certainly not be the person you would pick out of a group of people that you may guess experienced anything paranormal. As far as pub locals go, he was not one of the constant regulars either but still dropped in from time to time. I warmed to Roy, as I often find whilst investigating the paranormal that you discover many stories about places and people. Roy certainly had a good number of stories of his own, most not paranormal and many which would certainly make a good read. He was an interesting character for sure.

Leanne, Mat and I continued to watch the locals that evening as they enjoyed the Friday Night Karaoke at the Royal Oak, and how they continued to interact with each other. This brought us back to that nice feeling of family, which many of them seemed to display. Rachael was more than a landlady in all this too, she came across very much as that important family member as I previously mentioned.

Discussing what we were dealing with in this investigation, we wondered if the pub activity may have something to do with energies that appear to charge the place. However, potentially various types of energy, not the standard spiritual energy you may encounter with a haunted location. These would be equally associated to the people there now, and not just related to potential spirits roaming around the pub. It is hard to explain really, but our thought pattern was based on the energy that events like that evening's karaoke was generating amongst the locals and within the location itself. Perhaps it was this that assisted in influencing those that visited the Royal Oak into having paranormal experiences. It was really a very loose thought process which had little supporting evidence and certainly was more akin to a spiritual viewpoint rather than one we should pursue as investigators of the paranormal. However, I find it is important to theorise from time to time, but you have to remain mindful that you should still follow the evidence.

Soon enough, though, the evening came to an end and the locals reluctantly began to head home, each saying goodbye to one another, but especially to Rachael. Leanne, Mat and I had a coffee and catch-up with Rachael before heading up to bed. Although I am certain the catch-up progressed into the small hours. Whilst it was strange to be at a location in this way prior to our usual investigation approach, it was hugely helpful in gathering more understanding regarding the case itself. A case that was more than simply some noted paranormal activity, or a potentially haunted old pub; this case was beginning to help me recognise a connection between the people experiencing the activity, the location and activity itself. I was quickly beginning to realise the complexity here and that it was going to take more than one or two overnight investigations to help me comprehend the Royal Oak.

Due to travel and a few late nights, we woke up a little later than planned the following morning. Knowing that it would be a good idea to remove ourselves from the Royal Oak for a little while, we headed into town to find some breakfast and to begin to discuss the case. Also, we thought it a good opportunity to visit the seafront and drop into the Swanage Heritage Centre for a little research.

We managed to find a really nice cafe that served what we all agreed was a pretty tasty breakfast. It was also nice to briefly see the seafront and breathe in the sea air. We all agreed that it felt completely disconnected to the Royal Oak, even though we were very much still in Swanage. Swanage on that morning of Saturday, 8 June, 2013, felt like there was a certain bustle about it. Perhaps it was from the many seasonal visitors enjoying the good weather and seaside location.

The Heritage Centre was to be our main port of call and such a significant stop too. Following on from my discussion with Roy, we wondered about the large photograph on the wall near the gentlemen's toilets. It displayed several quarrymen, pictured in front of a quarry. The simple picture seemed very much like a stock photo but also carried with it an interesting element of familiarity. Some of the characters felt known or looked similar to a couple of the locals, but at that point we did not rule out the simple possibility that we just expected them to be and thus made the association.

In all honesty I did not think we would be able to locate the picture, based on my original assumption that it was some kind of stock photograph. If we did, it would certainly be quickly identified as such. However, on this occasion the very nice gentleman at the Heritage Centre was more than happy to go above and beyond to help us find it. Instantly he recognised it, which quickly ended my stock photograph theory. We managed to associate it with some other photographs taken at Belle Vue Quarry, now a farm. These also matched some in one of the Heritage Centre's displays. In fact, as I examined that display closer, I found a copy of our photograph.

The gentleman at the Centre continued to search for more information, but we were unable to locate it. However, this did not stop him, and we found ourselves heading off down the quay towards the Archives. He searched through yet more photographs, finally finding a cropped version and also another photograph of two of the men. This indicated that the photographs were taken at the Hanson Quarry, which is not too far from Swanage or the Royal Oak. Also, for an extra point, there were members of the Haysom family at the Royal Oak from 1885 to 1907.

Were the four gentlemen in the picture members of the Haysom family? Well, the photograph also dated around this time too. In fact, the photograph was from the Heritage Centre's Curator's personal collection. The Curator being one David Hanson, I believe.

We also managed to confirm that the photograph was most likely taken 2 September, 1896. However, we still could not fully identify the four men photographed. Around this time, Henry Haysom was at the Royal Oak. We all agreed that it was slightly odd that one of the men in the photograph resembled Roy a great deal. We took some copies of the photographs we had found that appear to link the large wall photograph to the Haysom family and their time at the Royal Oak.

Following our trip into town, we headed back to the Royal Oak and explained to Rachael what we had found. Then we took the opportunity to go in search of the quarry in question, but this time our search around the nearby countryside was unsuccessful. After what felt like such a promising lead, we returned to the pub around five.

On our return, we headed upstairs to our room to discuss the case further and plan out the investigation. However, it was not long before Rachael called us down to the bar area to meet Nick and Gina, who had just arrived. The couple would be joining us later that evening for our investigation, but we wanted to interview them ahead of the proceedings. Whilst they do frequent the pub quite regularly, they do not live locally, so it would be fair to say that they were a good example of individuals that whilst visiting Swanage had found themselves drawn to visit the pub, but then became regulars in a different way.

So, as Leanne and Mat prepared their cameras, I went down to the bar area to begin speaking with the couple. As I entered the bar, Rachael took me to where they were sitting, briefly introduced us and then basically told us to talk. I am not sure if Rachael takes this approach of saying as little as possible to ensure that she is not leading any conversations or because she is simply always very busy running the pub. Still, we managed introductions and at Rachael's suggestion headed to the dining room for the interview.

We sat and chatted briefly whilst we waited for Leanne and Mat. I had no reason to believe the couple were not genuine straight away. I also soon realised that their story was similar to so many others that Rachael had told me in relation to the pub.

My sister and Mat arrived in the dining room and set up ready for the interview. In the past I had pushed myself forward to do the interviewing, but this time around I just did not feel it was my role here. Without really thinking about it, I asked Leanne to interview the couple whilst I took notes in the background. Mat circled between us obtaining various camera angles of the interview. Leanne did an excellent job and perhaps this is her calling, to interview and document the stories I have begun to chase, but also other stories that people have and wish to share about their lives.

As for Nick and Gina, their story turned out to be quite interesting. Originally the couple were in Swanage for a break and were hiring a little cottage just down the road from the Royal Oak. As the closest pub to the cottage, they decided to drop in for a drink one day and it pretty much took off from there. Like many that I have spoken to about the Royal Oak, they both stated how much of a friendly welcoming place it was. Is it possible that this friendly, inviting atmosphere was why people were drawn to the pub or was there something else? Whilst it could easily be as simple as that, I do not think it was so back then or now.

The couple went on to explain how they spoke with Rachael early on and how she soon picked up that Gina was sensitive. This did not really surprise Gina, though, as she also told us that on her side of the family the women are sensitive to spirit. It is something she has understood as normal most of her life. Rachael also believed that Nick had spiritual connections too; this really shocked the pair. At that point Nick did not believe he was remotely sensitive.

Once acquainted to a satisfactory level, Rachael allowed the couple to explore the upstairs of the pub to see what they may pick up on. This is an action on Rachael's part which does seem to have become a regular invitation to those that she believes may have some connection with spirits.

During this exploration, the couple recalled that it was expected that Gina would pick up on a few things, which she certainly did. At first, I wondered if Rachael was somehow testing people that claimed to be sensitive by sending them into the depths of the pub to see what they might pick up and if it matched what she knew; nowadays, I genuinely believe that it was less of a test and more like she wanted to first gain more information from other sensitives on the oddities of the pub, and second, see if any of it may match up to the information she had already. However, as Gina and Nick approached Rachael's old bedroom on the first floor, now used as an office by Selwyn, one of the pub's long term tenants at the time, it was Nick that suddenly felt as if he could not enter the room.

Nick explained to us that it was as if something was preventing him from entering, which he really did not understand. They said that Rachael immediately understood, went in the room and removed a cap; this apparently changed something and allowed Nick to enter the room. If this event sounds a little odd, but equally somewhat dramatic, then you would be thinking along the same lines as I was. This scenario was not unique, and I am pretty sure that we encountered it a few more times over the years. It is equally not unique to the Royal Oak case either, as I have encountered it at other locations where sensitives have been unable to enter a room or area, attributing the block to an object of some kind. As an investigator you have to, with an open mind, theorise to what this may actually mean if indeed it means anything. The first thought is probably the most common, which is that this is fraud. Nick presented an inability to enter a particular room in order to raise the drama of the situation, then to provide some kind of justification for his actions; Rachael enters the room and identifies the cap as being the source of the fictional block. In order to add belief to his actions, Nick immediately agrees with Rachael that the cap is the source and with its removal the block has gone. If indeed these actions by both Nick and Rachael are to be considered fraudulent, then are we to suppose also that they constructed this story together or perhaps separately to gain trust. Keep in mind that at this point neither party had a reason to believe the other with regard to paranormal activity or capability. Equally, as stories of strangeness, this one is not the most thrilling I have heard, so why include it at all? If we are to believe this to be genuine then it would mean that an object could potentially contain energy of some kind that Nick detected, and that energy provided information enough for him to stop where he was going. Perhaps an object that Rachael was aware of, as she removed it to resolve the situation. There are stories and reports of objects having paranormal connections or even being haunted, in fact transference of information via objects about their past owners is something often practised by mediums.

Nick and Gina were at this point regular visitors to the Royal Oak since 2007. They said their first experience was like going home, time passed quickly and it was comfortable. It was not long before Rachael offered them a room at the pub, rather than staying elsewhere. It would be fair to say that the couple had become friends of Rachael and perhaps the pub too. Perhaps brought together by their similar interests in spirituality and the paranormal, or maybe the pub had brought them together for a reason.

As it was now obvious that the couple had spent some time at the pub, we wondered what they had experienced either together or individually. Gina immediately offered up a frightening experience that she had in the Poppy Room, located on the top floor of the pub. Gina advised that on this occasion she had headed up to the room to have a lie down on the bed. I can only assume, as my notes failed to capture the finer details, that this was during the day, most likely the afternoon. Whilst she lay on the double bed, she felt a pressure pushing down on her, preventing her from getting up. She soon realised that one of her arms was also outstretched and felt as if it was strapped to the bed. She thought that someone was present in the room with her and putting things into her arm. She told us that she was also aware of shadows moving around the room and also that someone was putting something into her neck. Gina told us it was a terrifying experience, which she had never felt previously.

Gina went on to tell us how she felt that someone had committed suicide in the room under Rachael's new bedroom, which is in the attic space where I experienced the pocket watch incident. She said that she also had the urge to sit in the window in that room.

Gina explained that when she and Nick stayed in the twin room on the top floor, they felt someone touching their legs. They described the feeling as oddly comfortable. I thought this was strange, because the only situation whereby someone touching your legs might feel comfortable could be a massage of some kind. My notes at the time do not appear to expand on this point, I wish I had now as it's an odd thing to describe. It is strange how we may miss such things at the time.

In 2011, when the couple stayed once again, Gina awoke one night in pain, in what she described as a "black mood" and as if she had been taken over by spirit. In all honesty, at the time I was unsure what to make of this comment. I'm unsure if it was an experience at all or simply Gina just waking up in a bad mood. Again, I wish I had explored this a little more.

The couple also reported that they had seen a very different style of garden from the Poppy Room window. Gina particularly explained that sometimes she will only see fields and none of the houses that currently exist behind the Royal Oak. This experience was something that caught my interest, as it highlighted something that had already begun to present itself within the story of the Royal Oak: time!

This theme was again presented in another one of Gina and Nick's stories, where time had changed on their mobile phone. A change that could not happen by accident, as it required access to several menus to make the change. The couple advised that the mobile phone had changed to 01:20 on 13 March, 2010; this was particularly odd in relation to the Royal Oak as it was the year and day of the start of the garden wall falling down as advised by Rachael. I thought that this was a coincidence because earlier that day, a pocket watch that I had taken to the pub had also changed its time by an hour, it advanced one hour and stopped! Had the pocket watch advanced one hour or was I also reading strange coincidences into seemingly normal occurrences. I decided that it would be something to keep an eye on.

Whilst in the living room area on the first floor, the couple reported that they felt something rush past them. An odd feeling of something making its presence known, when there was nothing to be seen. Nick also advised of his pint being tipped over, as if a child was attempting to taste his beer, something which I assume occurred in the bar area.

As the interview progressed, we decided to try and understand what spirits were to be encountered at the pub. Gina spoke of a girl with long dark hair down her back. She then mentioned a second girl with a ponytail or pigtails in her hair, but that spirit is one that prefers to hide. One of her hiding places is behind the bar, where she can be a little naughty as she likes messing about. Gina stated that she may be around seven or eight years old.

Also, behind the bar, near to the washup area, Gina described a woman that would appear there sometimes. The spirit of the woman would smile nicely at Gina, but when she moved her hair, she would reveal a rope around her neck. Then suddenly, Gina would perceive a vision of the woman hanging herself! When she witnessed this, Gina was sat at the bar, so it obviously shocked her initially. Not something you generally expect to witness whilst having a drink at a quiet little pub, but something that I suppose was fast becoming the norm at the Royal Oak.

The couple made an interesting statement about how the Royal Oak changed according to the day and how Rachael was too. I wondered if this may be partially related to time or even historical events echoing on the present, and equally if that may also impact Rachael somehow. There was certainly more to this case potentially than that of a haunting, as it appeared to have so much more of a storyline occurring. One which seemed oddly entangled with Rachael's own life story. Whether it was possible for such things to occur, I was not sure, especially in such a way that it may have a strange connection to the landlady, who appeared destined to be there. It even made me consider the relevance of our involvement and our presence; were we now becoming entangled in the story of the Royal Oak?

Nick then described his trance mediumship experience at the Royal Oak, beginning with "you need to be open minded about it all" and as such we were, so as readers of this, I hope you are too. On this occasion Nick had come to Swanage to take it easy following an injury to his hand. At the time he was sat at the bar, near the pump. He advised that it was at this point he felt something odd, as if spirit was coming through. Whilst he does not remember it too well at all, he said he felt physical pain and was told that he spoke to Rachael. It is believed that a local who had passed away, called Gary, came through Nick and at the time there was even a slight facial change too.

The next time that Nick would go into trance, he said, that Rachael was also in trance. He advised that he was told that while he was in trance he looked smaller and different to others, like an old man. What was also bizarre was that his voice appeared to be very small too. This odd concept of spirit channelling through him to the degree where they could alter the perception of how he looked and sounded appeared to confuse Nick. To be fair at that point it confused me. The only time I had witnessed transfiguration, the complete change of appearance or form, it had been very obviously fraudulently done using a light, but what Nick was talking about was an individual's physical form appearing very different to others. This was something that interested me at the time, especially as there also seemed to be some variations of mental and trance mediumship occurring at the Royal Oak. It was also interesting that eighteen months previously Nick did not really believe these things were possible, certainly not the things he now appeared to be capable of, but it would appear according to his statements, that he had developed at great speed.

One thing that really caught my attention was that the couple both stated that they just could not keep away from the Royal Oak now. When they feel that they have to be at the pub, they find that they must just go! Each time they do, something happens. It is as if they can have all their experiences at the Royal Oak and then can leave it behind. Something I found quite interesting as it almost presented the pub as somewhere they would go to gain their spiritual or paranormal fix before returning to their normal lives. A concept that I thought could be relatively dangerous too, as such a concept could be seen as an addiction and those never work out well.

As the interview with the couple began to head towards a close, we picked up on some similar fundamentals from others. Nick and Gina commented on how they thought there was a much bigger key story around Rachael. This comment did not shock me, as many have made this connection and also began to link it to past lives. In this case the past lives appear to be those connected to the pub back in Victorian times. The couple compared it to a jigsaw puzzle. Adding the "pub picks who it wants there" which I found a little dramatic and potentially a little Hollywood for my liking. Still, I could not deny that there was an odd story evolving here that seemed to define the pub as a beacon for those with paranormal gifts, drawing them in to visit once, but where they would then remain friends for longer. I had to wonder if that included me as an investigator too. The couple certainly stated that you can feel linked to the pub and people will know when you are only a few miles away, understanding that you would walk through the door shortly. They also mentioned a little about energy and how certain individuals help the spiritual energy of the pub, and that there are spirits looking over Rachael's shoulder, keeping an eye on things.

Whilst this may seem both sinister and somewhat dramatic, it's not really their opinion alone, other locals have equally made statements that are similar to this during my investigation of the Royal Oak. As an investigator I was beginning to wonder what I was investigating here: a simple haunted old pub or something much more. The pub was presenting itself as being haunted, but with the strange ability to connect with people that have paranormal gifts like mediumship. Equally, the comments around the more dramatic story relating to Rachael and the pub drawing in these people whose specific energy helped to gain a greater spiritual connection was like something straight out of the movies to me. I suspected there may be a logical explanation, but it may take some finding.

Later on that day, Anne and Dawn, members of my team that I had asked to join us, arrived outside the pub. I met them prior to them entering the pub and took them straight through into the garden. I wanted to keep them apart from everyone, as I needed them to try and pick up on anything first because they were both individuals that are sensitive to spirit. This means that they can both pick up on various pieces of information a little like a medium, but not quite as focussed as a medium. However, in some recent investigations and experiments, their involvement had been very useful in connecting with the potential spirit activity that this investigator struggles to tune into.

Rachael, Mat and Leanne soon joined us in the garden, but Rachael ensured that she did not let anything slip. Once again solidifying that she potentially just wanted answers the same as I did. After some formal introductions, we headed back into the pub and up to the Poppy Room. Although this was only to drop off our stuff before heading down the road to the local fish and chip shop to grab some dinner.

Walking Anne and Dawn up through the various levels of the building, I could tell that at least Anne was picking up on something already. However, rather than diving in at that point, I decided to leave it alone for a while and give them the chance to acclimatise first. Working with those sensitive to spirit and mediums over the years, I have learned to be mindful of them when in potentially haunted locations, as sometimes some of them can quickly become overwhelmed. The solution for this situation is nearly always for them to leave the location fully, allowing them to disconnect. I wonder if it is as if they just receive an abundance of information all in one go, which is difficult for them to process. For me, this presents two possibilities: the first is that there are spirits who are all trying to communicate at once, the second being that there are so many environmental triggers that their minds are downloading an abundance of information telepathically. Of course, both these possibilities rest on something supernormal rather than another explanation found more in the realms of normality.

After a brief chat we headed downstairs and as we reached the first floor, I decided to ask Anne what she had picked up. Knowing Anne reasonably well at that point, I could tell when she was picking something up and I wanted her confidence to build early to ensure that she would engage completely in the events later on. Often on other investigations, Anne had sensed things, but rather than confidently provide that information within the moment she had kept it to herself and provided it to me individually later on. However, for the investigation, I really wanted to gain as much information as possible, so wanted her to let me know as soon as she had something. I was not surprised to learn that she had picked up on a spirit of a young girl aged approximately seven or eight years old, with curly dark hair. This description fitted others I had heard before from the pub's locals. I saw immediately that Anne had become more confident and as such would be happier to engage with us all.

For some reason unknown to me, I knew that Anne was a very capable medium who has developed beyond her own belief in herself. She often remains quiet in the background to enable her to investigate using her sensitivity to spirit but also share what she knows with others like Dawn, who at this time felt very much like Anne's apprentice.

We left the Royal Oak for a while, and I took the opportunity to discuss my plan with Anne and Dawn, hoping that they may understand my approach. They confirmed to me that they were the right people for the investigation at that point in time, something I did not truly understand. I had a strange feeling of knowing who the right people would be, which was completely against my usual approach to investigating; however, I wanted to embrace more of the spiritual approach on this occasion, as it was extremely important to the locals and the location itself.

Returning to the Royal Oak, we sat down in the dining room and relaxed into conversation, catching up, swapping paranormal stories and generally getting comfortable in the place. The relevance of this socialising aspect of the evening was not obvious to me at that point in time, but now I truly understand how important it may have been. We had already stepped away from our usual firmly structured approach and were embracing the relaxing atmosphere of the pub. As I look back on the events of that time at the Royal Oak and perhaps others too, as with any process or even ritual, there may be certain things you simply cannot leave out. It certainly seems to me that the social engagement, whilst not always obviously connected to an investigation at the Royal Oak, is most certainly always there in some shape or form. If we think about this for a moment, it seems reasonable to assume it would be considering the location is a pub where locals have gathered in such a way for many a century now. Perhaps the purported hauntings even stem from this social energy that the place creates. Whatever it may be, it's certainly relevant in some way.

As we sat in the dining room, time passed by relatively quickly, the evening was beginning to get away from us already and we still had some preparation work to do. We headed through the "fun house" construction of the Royal Oak to re-group in the Poppy Room. Following a group discussion, we took the decision to set up the camera system, so they covered anything on the two staircases and out in the garden. Oddly for me on this occasion, I was not worried about capturing anything on film; the experience itself would be sufficient. However, Leanne had convinced me to set them up any way, just in case.

By the time the Royal Oak had closed its doors on Saturday, 8 June, 2013, my team and I had set up a few closed-circuit TV cameras around the property. The remaining locals were gathered in the bar area, as my team of five joined them. It was one of those moments as I do not believe any of us really knew what to expect of the rest of our night. It was not like any investigation that I had previously conducted with my team, especially as we would be working with the locals on this one. It was even stranger because the locals were also various individuals that had experienced the oddities of the Royal Oak previously and they would now be participating in our investigation of their claims.

As we all were in the bar area, I broke the awkwardness by instigating the introductions of the teams so that everyone got to know each other before we proceeded. There were fourteen of us present in total, but I was convinced there would only be thirteen. I had mentioned this to Rachael a few times, so was a little surprised for us to be one over. With me was Leanne, Mat, Dawn and Anne; and with Rachael were Terri, Mo, Pete, Nick, Gina, John, Jan and Roy.

My original plan was to group together and take a walk around the upstairs of the pub, but fourteen people walking around the pub was not going to work for that space. With this we split into two groups, and I led the first group up to the living room area. I believe the group consisted of me, Leanne, Mat, Dawn, Terri, and Mo. In previous visits to the pub various things had been picked up, and that night the group were sensitive to this right away. Some of the known haunting stories came through quite quickly. However, it was the Poppy Room on the second floor that truly had an impact on the group: Mo slipped into trance, complaining of a problem with his throat! It was interesting as I had never seen this kind of mediumship first hand. At the time I took it at face value and did not attempt to question it too much, especially as it was the very experience we were looking for at the pub. As this session was quite energy consuming for Mo, I decided to head back to the bar area afterwards.

I then took the second group of Mat, Anne, Rachael, Pete, Nick, Gina, John, Jan, and Roy upstairs to the same rooms again to see what they may pick up. Once again, the group picked up on things right away. Incidentally Roy seemed to complain about every room he entered, but it was Rachael's bedroom at that time that really made him react badly. He seemed upset and almost as if it was hard for him to enter the room. When he did, he stated that it was the room from one of his dreams where the roof beam struck a woman's head and killed her. This thought upset him, and he left with Rachael's assistance.

Oddly he felt at ease in Rachael's old bedroom, the one that Nick told us he had trouble with previously until a hat was removed.

We headed to the Poppy Room and Roy found that he could not enter, again as Nick had described previously, he was blocked from entering. Whilst we were in the room, some of us could smell what we could only describe as a kind of hospital disinfectant. At this point I would like to say that I did not smell it too, but I cannot; the smell was as obvious to me as it was to the others in the group and very distinct. I recalled Gina's earlier story of her feeling strapped to the bed. I wondered if the two things could be connected and if they were, how?

Crossing the small hallway, we passed the galleried stairs and entered the twin bedroom. We sat down to see what might come through. Rachael advised us that she picked up on a woman in the corner of the room. However, as I was discussing this with Rachael, Roy was obviously becoming increasingly uncomfortable. Then, all of a sudden, Roy screamed angrily, "Why don't you fuck off out the pub?"

This took us all a little by surprise. I think Rachael asked who it was as we did not believe it was Roy communicating with us. Roy replied, "You fucking know me!"

At this point Rachael, Pete and Nick ended the session by leaving the room, turning the lights on and getting Roy to leave the room. As they escorted Roy from the room he looked totally confused by their actions and his response reminded me of someone that had just recovered from an epileptic seizure. In fact, as an epileptic that suffered from such things in my teenage years, I can completely understand Roy's reaction. You feel as if you've lost time, that events have passed and although you were present, you have no recollection of them at all. For Roy, it was not until he got to the stairs that he was fully back with us and aware of where he was. We decided to re-group in the bar area to deconstruct what had just occurred.

However, at that point something particularly strange came to pass for me, something that I actually contemplated leaving out of this book, but then I would not be honest and could be considered to be withholding information about the case itself. So, after much deliberation I have decided to include my thoughts on this event as they were then in 2013. My initial thought, as odd as it was back then, was that the probable entity that had communicated through Roy may have been Andrew! It is important to note that I have literally no evidence to support this thought process other than a random feeling I had at the time. It was a thought that troubled me greatly, because I did not know how to approach this with Rachael. In case it is not clear, Andrew is the same person I had met at the Royal Oak and was very much alive.

Later that night, I would find the time and hopefully the right words to discuss this with Rachael and, oddly, she agreed. She said that he had not been invited but may have possibly wanted to be there that night. Rachael said that she was not sure how he may have achieved it, but it could be similar to astral projection. So, whilst in a relaxed state, which could either be during meditation or simply whilst asleep, Andrew's spirit could have left his physical body, travelled through the astral plain and found itself at the pub where it took control of Roy. It was something as far-fetched as a Hollywood movie script, but, oddly, not something I could readily dismiss in that moment.

After years of research and experience, the possession of Roy in the twin bedroom still sits clearly in my mind. The experiences that occurred are what I consider a pivotal moment now as they indicate an event or point in time that has the potential for multiple possible explanations. The first we must obviously entertain as investigators is that of fraud. I had little knowledge of Roy and on that night he simply acted as if he had become possessed, making the whole event an elaborate drama for our benefit. However, like many situations at the Royal Oak, when we evaluate them for fraud there appears to be little value for the individual or the pub. The same was true here; Roy was an infrequent local at the Royal Oak and not looking to become a famous medium of some kind. Equally his actions provided no bearing on the Royal Oak, nor did they bring financial gain or fame. Also, there were no specifics about the event, it was an outburst, plain and simple. The second is an area I don't believe I am qualified to comment upon in detail, which is the area of psychology. I am unaware of Roy's psychiatric state as a professional may be, but from my own interactions with him he seemed as reasonably balanced as any of the locals. He did not display any obvious issues to us. Certainly nothing that could be associated with a potential secondary personality that may emerge whilst we were conducting our investigation.

As the group swapped stories in the bar area, I began the next phase of the night's plan. However, it is probably fair to mention that "in my head" the initial walk around the pub was not to investigate or allow both the locals and my team to bond. In my head, I saw the team walk around as an important method to assist in the process before we could conduct a seance. Oddly, the simplest way I can describe this is that it is like the final wind of a pocket watch! A bit like linking the individuals with the location in order to prime them both. I really have no idea why this feels how it should be done; it is just something I feel is right. I have always felt that it is important to be open minded whilst investigating the paranormal, and to be open to methods and approaches that may not always seem logical or scientific. However, this does not mean that whilst attempting these strange approaches you should not remain observant and mindful of the events occurring around you. If anything, you have to be more so in order to recognise potential information or actions that may be considered important to the case. These could, of course, be fraudulent acts or indeed small pieces of information that provide potential evidence.

As we were setting up the chairs around the table in the dining room, Rachael popped her head in, as she wanted to discuss Roy with me. Following the episode in the twin room she felt (as did I) that he may not be ready for what we were about to try. With this understanding we spoke to Roy and convinced him that it may be best for him to head off home. Whatever had happened to Roy in the twin room, it had now become the catalyst for us asking him to leave. If indeed it was fraudulent then in my opinion it now had an adverse effect, as he would no longer be present for the main part of the night. At that point, though, I did not believe it was fraud as Roy left willingly, perhaps concerned himself what may occur next and equally Rachael was happy for him to go. There were now only thirteen people remaining to be seated at the seance. Around the table there was one empty chair, matching my original design. Whilst this may sound dramatic, it could be stated that this was always going to be achieved somehow, as we had already made up our minds that we would have thirteen and as such made the choice to send Roy home in order to achieve this.

With everyone's place organised, the next step was to add the subconscious triggers, which had been picked to hopefully have the group expand their connectivity, maybe without even realising it. These I refer to as the spirit team, a name originally used by the Scole Experiment back in the nineties. To be honest this was something I wanted to keep, perhaps to help bind some kind of connection, if that was possible. Leanne, Mat and I also threw in a few extra names of our family members. I am not exactly sure why we did this, perhaps we all hoped for a connection of our own to someone that we had lost over the years, someone we knew and could easily confirm through minimal information provided. The names were written on a conveniently placed whiteboard for all to see prior to the lights being turned off.

Leanne set up a camera to record the first hour of the seance, before its battery would expire. I was not keen on the camera being present on this occasion as I thought that it may hinder things slightly. Either through individuals being unable to relax totally or through its infra-red light, which had been said to cause issues over the year. I struggled with the presence of infra-red cameras as it seemed that in these cases where a camera was present with the ability to see in the dark, activity diminished. To state that the one thing that may catch evidence of fraud was also the object stopping activity made no sense. Still, as with much in the paranormal, evidence is still pending in either direction. So, on that occasion we decided to have a camera present that would turn off after a certain amount of time. I have a feeling that as a side experiment, we could have advised that it only had thirty minutes remaining or something, however, I do not believe the group appeared particularly bothered by its presence.

With our seance room all set up and ready to go, I headed out into the bar area and invited everyone into the dining room. As they entered the room, I told them where to sit and made them aware of the whiteboard full of names. Everyone sat down, got comfortable, and we turned the lights out. At this point, much to the confusion of some, I handed over control to Terri and

Rachael, as it was their spiritual circle. After all, I was only a guest too.

Terri began by grounding us all, then inviting us all to meditate slightly. This was the kind of meditation, from what I can remember, where you would visualise yourself in a nice place, say walking through the woods or a meadow. After a few minutes had passed, and we had returned from our personal meditation, Terri asked each of us in turn about our experience. One by one, each of us around the table began to share our own method of meditation and the experience that we had during it.

However, before we made it fully around the table, Mo slipped into trance and began to channel a spirit. We quickly recognised this as he laughed out loud oddly, a sign that Rachael had pointed out to us earlier when he was connecting to his spirit guides.

The first few communicators did not stay long, each saying very little before passing on, perhaps made to leave by Mo's guide, the Japanese man. Then a communicator who seemed oddly familiar to us began to come through clearly, although I really am unable to confirm how this was. The first thing I recall the communicator saying (through Mo) was "interesting". It is equally important to mention that the voice we heard was certainly not that of Mo's normal voice. In fact, it was dramatically different! I wondered if it was the first word spoken by this voice that I recognised? Terri took the opportunity to ask the name of our visiting communicator, and he identified himself as William. With this I looked at my sister and realised that she was paying attention now, even though she appeared a little defensive, possibly as she was sat right next to Mo. Terri then added to this by asking the communicator where he had come from.

The communicator replied, "Enfield."

With this response, my sister obviously made an association to our grandfather on my father's side, and she became overwhelmed with emotion. Oddly, the communicator reacted to this by claiming that he came with love, but more importantly he then asked Leanne if she was okay. In fact, the communicator called William appeared genuinely concerned about Leanne and reached out (through Mo) to comfort her. Was this the spirit of our grandfather? Whilst I would like to think so, there remains insufficient evidence to support a positive identification of the communicator. This may seem a little harsh, but I have read of communicators that have presented themselves through mediums to members of the SPR and provided so much information that their identity was without question. Still, it was an interesting first communication, equally something I was not completely ready for even though my grandfather's name was on the whiteboard.

Shortly after this, the communicator called William moved on; once again a few more attempted to come through unsuccessfully. Terri continued to talk to Mo as he returned from his trance, ensuring that all was well with him and that he was fully out of trance before leaving him alone. One thing was completely evident about this group, they looked after one another well. This was something which obviously brought them closer and likely added to their spiritual circle. As Mo returned to us, he drank two pints of water at great speed.

Terri continued to ask around the table regarding our meditation experiences. At this point I felt comfortable to add my own odd experience. Whilst I did not really meditate exactly, as I have always had a little trouble with that, what I did have was a clear voice in my mind telling me to remove my cap. It was clear to me that it was asking me to do so, as it was rude to be wearing one. Initially I thought it was me somehow, but the voice repeated a few times until I physically removed my cap. It was certainly a strange one to mention, and whilst I did feel a little silly telling everyone of this, it felt good to share it. Looking back, I could probably explain it as the voice being my own consciousness recognising the event had formality to it and as such wearing a cap would be considered rude. Whilst I am not advocating that a spirit was telling me to do this, I have to admit I felt compelled so much so that I actually removed my cap. Of course, if not a spirit or my own sub-conscious, this may have been the thoughts of someone else at the table telepathically received. There are several possibilities here, but the fact is simple, at that point in time I removed my cap, something I would not usually have done.

I believe that Mo slipped into trance a few more times, but no communicators came through as dramatically and clearly as William from Enfield had. Then things went quiet for a little while and other methods of connecting were attempted. During this time, the name Walter came up from a member of the group (pub locals), which was said to be related to a whistle. The number seven came up twice, as did the month September; perhaps these would become more apparent later?

Then without warning we recognised that Rachael was acting a little odd. As Dawn and I watched her she said "quill" then slipped into her own trance. Again, Terri asked the spirit's name, to which Rachael replied or rather tried to reply, saying "Tom" or "John", we were not sure which one. However, at that point the communicator appeared to be having great trouble communicating through Rachael. However, she did appear to be taking something out of her pocket and checking it. Whilst some of the group questioned her action trying to determine what she was doing, I knew she was checking a pocket watch. Instinctively, I passed her my grandfather's (on my mother's side) pocket watch. She held it and became a little emotional. She pointed to the watch, looking for us to possibly guess her message. We assumed she meant "time" or "times", to which she agreed. Then she proceeded to draw a cross in the air; we asked if she meant "cross". She agreed and held up two fingers to signify "two".

The message was "two times cross", albeit somewhat cryptic and a little like charades.

In my head, I believed I knew what this may mean, or perhaps what it may mean to me. It simply means that two timelines crossed. In this case the past and the present. It was what we had managed to do that night. I am not sure if anyone else understood the message in the same way, but shortly following the delivery of this message, Rachael came out of trance unaware of what had transpired.

Terri then mentioned the whistle again and this time directed focus onto Mat, who I think was deemed to be the most sceptical of the group. Whether that was true or not, I was not sure as I had not really had the time to discuss the subject at length with him to understand where exactly he may stand belief wise. As this discussion about the whistle continued, some of us thought that Gina had fallen asleep, however, that was certainly not the case! Terri quickly associated the whistle with the name Walter. However, in that moment the focus seemed to be on the whistle which the group believed was associated with a train whistle, or perhaps a training whistle or similar. It was clear that Terri and potentially a few others that were sensitive were picking up on something that was related to this whistle. Suddenly, from nowhere, Gina wolf-whistled, which was shockingly loud in the little dining room but also sounded exactly like the whistle of a steam train. This clarified to the group that Gina had slipped into trance herself unknown to us and had begun to channel a probable spirit. The personality of the communicator was struggling to communicate and some of the group made the suggestion that they may possibly be on the autism spectrum. Labelling this communicator with a possible mental health issue was in my opinion a leap. I wondered if this was something they were sensing about the communicator or even Mat himself. Still, I felt there was more to this than met the eye. I also had a feeling based on the communication so far that there was someone else. Terri attempted to make contact with the communicator, and they oddly advised us that where they were it was daytime. It was certainly strange to experience such things, and before we knew it Gina was slipping out of trance. She angrily screamed "no" again making us all jump a little. The group of locals decided that at this point it was a good idea to bring Gina fully out of trance; Terri eventually assisted with this. However, this was not to be an easy return to our reality, Gina did not seem okay as she came out of trance. At this point, we made the decision to close the spiritual circle and seance, which was done with a prayer.

Mo then slipped into trance during this closing phase and his communicator quickly delivered a part of the prayer. Terri asked Mo if he was okay. He responded with "yes", but then followed up with "but I would be lying". This was a little chilling, to be fair. That was not the end of it though, whilst Gina was still in trance, several of us saw an odd light anomaly which we described as an arm behind her. Initially I thought it was Leanne, but she denied it and her sleeves were down. The apparitional arm could be seen from mid-way up the forearm to the hand. It was very, very odd.

As the spiritual circle broke and the group began to discuss the events, some of which I may have missed, it was then that I realised that Gina was not herself and not fully out of trance! A strange association to famous medium Helen Duncan was also made at this point, but there is, of course, a lack of information to qualify it, making it hard to pursue such a claim. However, in the interest of safety I told Rachael, who immediately took Gina aside to assist her with coming out of trance. This was followed by a cleansing for us all, by Terri.

The entire group must have continued to talk about the events of the seance for nearly an hour afterwards. In fact, the seance had lasted several hours, taking it through to first light. Most of the guests then made their way home, leaving those of us sleeping at the Royal Oak to head up to bed. However, my team quickly took down the CCTV system first and packed our ghost hunting gadgets away.

My own night was not to end there, though; before heading off to sleep, I sat down with Rachael to talk things through and try and gain an understanding of the events that had transpired. Early on in the conversation, we discussed my grandfather's pocket watch, the relevance of time and why I was so particular about where people should be sat. This was an oddity, as I still struggle to explain it. It felt like an electrical circuit to me that required the right people in the right places to make it work. A strange, and seemingly more spiritual understanding perhaps that did not really conform to my usual understanding of the paranormal. What was equally odd about this was that I knew Rachael was in possession of her grandfather's pocket watch too; we felt it odd that we both had their watches with us. I tried to rationalise this, but it is possible that many grandfathers owned pocket watches. However, I felt something was inherently connected with it.

However, Rachael also randomly mentioned that the one other item of her grandfather's that she wanted was his medals. Initially I thought the medals to be from the war, but Rachael's response shocked me! The medals were from working on the buses, similar medals which I had recently received from my mother belonging to my grandfather. It also became apparent that both my and Rachael's grandfathers had served in similar places during the Second World War. I asked his name to check later, and Rachael responded with Sidney Frank Grant. The similarities between us were odd and I think we both believe there to be some reason for this, what it is escapes us both.

Tired and with the sun fully up outside, I went up to bed; well my space on the floor in the Poppy Room. Although sleeping was not easy and I had to talk briefly to Leanne, it was not too long before I managed to drift off to sleep. The events of the previous night remained prominent in my mind as they always do when I investigate as ever more questions were formulating than I had answers to. Another common trait of paranormal investigations is that if you are lucky enough to obtain one or two answers, then you will receive at least ten more questions. The overall answer always being just that little bit out of reach.

The morning of Sunday, 9 June, 2013, came far too soon for any of us and I think to some extent, we were all still a little shocked by the night's events. We all made it down to the bar area with our bags, almost ready to leave. However, we held on for a little while longer to grab a coffee and talk together about our experiences.

However, all in all it was a feeling of slight amazement with regard to the events that had transpired, but also we were all willing to embrace the experience as it was and not over think it too much. Even those of us that may still seek logic and science to explain things took on board that we had all just shared something quite extraordinary. I knew that only those present or that had experiences similar to ours would truly understand our enthusiasm, whilst others may shadow it with negativity and logical, possible explanations. Still, we left the Royal Oak that Sunday morning charged with a life-changing experience. Perhaps the events of the night had clarified where I would take my exploration of the paranormal next, but at that point I still was not sure of my own part in all this.

As we left, Rachael spoke to a few members of my team with regard to their spiritual ability, confirming that Anne should keep at it as her confidence was getting there and she was really good. I think Rachael also spoke to Dawn too, but I do not know what was said. Rachael also drew attention to my sister Leanne that she had a psychic ability and provided her with some comfort around this. However, there was nothing like this for me, we just said our goodbyes and she invited me back again anytime.

With that everyone else headed into Swanage for breakfast and to see the sea, as you cannot really visit a seaside town and not take two minutes to stop and look at it. On this occasion though, I left the team to it and began the long trip home, but I was constantly thinking about everything that had occurred during the previous night.

When I joined the M27, a strange design appeared in my mind along with a lot of information! It was like a sudden download hitting my mind all at once and even when I tried to clear my mind of it, this information dominated my thoughts. I tried to attribute it to a lack of sleep and even considered momentary madness; after all I was seeing complex designs in my head, and it did not stop there either. I also knew that the design seemed to me like a machine! It also had something to do with time or more specifically timelines. These timelines were in reference to the past, the present and the future. It also involved crossing those timelines or converging them at a single point in space and time! What was equally odd was that I knew this information and, also, that I thought it was right! In fact, I was so sure it was right that I pulled over at the next service station to ring Rachael. When I did, things became very weird. Rachael seemed to understand what I was saying, and also took it as gospel, not questioning any of it. I think I was actually hoping that she would tell me I was imagining it all, but she did not. In fact, she even added some extra parts which also made sense to me too! I continued to describe what I saw and knew, but could not show her the design until later when I arrived home.

I have to admit, from this point forward everything felt one hundred per cent different to me. I began to think there was more for me there at the Royal Oak, possibly something spiritual. My head seemed to be working overtime for the rest of the journey trying to understand this information, trying to rationalise it. At that point I can only describe it as if it was like a virus that perhaps the rest of my logical mind was attempting to deal with.

For example, why did I see three pocket watches at specific points on the design? Although at this point, I knew of three, possibly four. My grandfather's and my own pocket watch. Also, Rachael's grandfather's and the other one that she had too. In my mind, it was the two pocket watches from my and Rachael's grandfathers which were important here. Again, how I knew this, or even if it was right, is beyond me!

One other thing, which may have been inspired by the Scoles Experiment, was the presence of a glass jar in the centre of the design. Something which made me think that perhaps this was a design for a tabletop. I do question myself over this due to the influence of the Scole Experiment being ever present in my mind. However, I knew what I saw and knew somehow that energy could be channelled through it to obtain some interesting results.

There was one last piece to add to the puzzle on that Sunday, though. Whilst driving home, I had been phoned by the Swanage Heritage Centre in reference to the picture we had been looking into previously. They left me a voicemail with some interesting information. Dave Foster had made the call with David Hanson present as he was asked a couple of questions during the call. The enlarged photo at the Royal Oak was taken at Hanson's Quarry on 2 September, 1896, and was copied from a photograph in David Hanson's personal collection. However, the four men in the photograph were completely unknown. This was a shame as Rachael and indeed others at the Royal Oak seem interested in who these men were. Oddly though to me, the date seemed more important. Perhaps due to the obvious link to time once again, as this whole thing appears to be linked to time somehow!

When I arrived home, I emailed Dave Foster and David Hanson for further pictures from that time and hoped that the identification of the four men might eventually present itself. However, I do not believe I ever received a reply. Are the names of these men important? I am sure that Roy would believe so, as one was in his dreams. Not to mention the odd similarities between Roy and one of the four men, from a physical perspective.

There was one other thing I saw on Saturday night during the seance, that Mo's face physically appeared to change at times. This transmogrification seemed to occur around five times in possibly less than a minute! I also thought I witnessed the glasses on the table move at one point, but I am unable to find anyone else who witnessed the same. As such I must potentially see this as a trick of the light.

The events of the seance continued to remain with me following its completion; they had certainly had an impact on my understanding and experience of the paranormal. However, I was still trying to build a better picture of the situation. I desperately wanted to solve this mystery, and it was quickly growing into a rather complex one that was for sure.

On Sunday, 30 June, 2013, I wrote in my journal that since the seance, things for me have changed! At times in that first week following the seance, I felt as if my head might explode! I found myself, for the very first time, seeking guidance from mediums. You see, I was of the understanding that I was an outsider looking in on this world of the paranormal, but now I felt very much involved. Those whom I have spoken to, called it being "switched on" to this spiritual viewpoint, which I found a little ironic. However, all of a sudden, things that sounded a little crazy out loud actually made perfect sense to me. Most of them even seemed like something I already knew!

The information that I knew about, like how to set up and run the seance, was something I worked out but also sort of knew about. I also knew there would be only 13 people around the table. I knew that where Mo, Rachael and Terri sat was important, as they sat in a triangle! More importantly, I knew that time was very prominent to this whole situation. I already had an understanding of timelines prior to the seance. It seems as if the locals link the relevance of time to themselves and the Royal Oak. However, I believed it had greater meaning that needed further exploration, such as including direct relationships to the Royal Oak. After all, Ann picked up on Rachael being at the Royal Oak in a past life. You see, even the understanding of this meant a change within me. The events of our time at Swanage played heavily on my mind that first week after the event. It was a true enlightening and something I really could not ignore. Looking back over my time investigating the paranormal, I soon realised the relevance of my own path and how I had to begin to understand certain aspects prior to this, just to ensure that I experienced it and understood it correctly.

My investigations have given me some video evidence, audio evidence and lots of personal and shared experiences over the years. The point of the subjective evidence was to allow me to understand that it is not all about capturing evidence. The problem with what is understood to be paranormal evidence is that it is not always accepted within the wider community. Basically, unless someone was present when the evidence (video, picture or audio) is captured then they will always question it, and quite rightly so; I would do so myself. It took me a while to understand, but when I did it all seemed to make more sense. The only way to truly understand the paranormal is to experience it yourself. Every personal experience is different and enlightening in its own way. Although I did not fully understand this before heading to Swanage, I knew the approach to take had to be one that trusted in the experience and not just focussed on capturing the usual evidence.

This approach of going with the experience took shape at Bradwell Abbey, pretty much by accident really, when I sat in the small chapel with five sensitives and then heard a voice answer a few questions in my head! If that sounds more like I was going a little crazy, than a proper investigation, then I had similar thoughts. Perhaps I was developing psychic abilities similar to the sensitives present, or perhaps not. Either way, the experience certainly triggered something within me, which may not have been the gift of psychic powers but was certainly a new thought process, perhaps. Possibly a greater understanding of the paranormal, but more importantly it had opened the door to considering the spiritual side of the paranormal.

Suffice to say, I arrived in Swanage with a completely different outlook to that which I had during the June investigation of the Royal Oak. I think it was Pete who really hit the nail on the head when he said, "You're different, you've really done your homework!"

Perhaps he was right, as my experiments this time were about to push the boundaries of the unknown. How would this be achieved during this investigation, by contacting spirits that were possibly interested in spiritual exploration when they were alive? Why? So that we could have their assistance on "the other side", similar to the approach explored during the Scole Experiment. This would allow us to unite or cross the timelines! As slightly odd as this may sound, it made sense to me and is also reflected in the continued link to time potentially.

During this initial seance, I hoped to allow us to connect to one of the spirit team I put together that assisted in making a success of this approach. While no solid confirmation was really received, we did connect with someone from Enfield and not local to Swanage, which was unusual. They also picked up on a lot to do with Mat's grandfather. In my mind, I also feel that Gina channelled the medium Helen Duncan, but this is more of a gut feeling and there is no evidence of any kind to support this theory.

Still, this was the proof I needed to be sure that those at the Royal Oak were ready to begin on a greater level. Oddly, this all made perfect sense to me and I even knew certain pieces regarding time which is a little strange to be honest! When talking about time, we often understand it as the past has happened, we are living the present and the future has yet to be written. It may not be as linear as we experience it.

Rather than observing time as the passing of hands on a clock or as dates on a calendar, we should see it as constantly active timelines, presenting a possibly infinite number for the past, present and future. Each potentially bound to a variable such as a location or an individual, or perhaps both. I had these ideas just after the investigation, after having the experiences previously mentioned. Being a difficult concept to explain well, probably required me to think it through and simplify it somehow.

There are three primary timelines that we know of: the past, the present and the future. In order to cross these timelines, one would require certain individuals that can "tune in" to other timelines. Communication with other timelines could be seen as a connection with the spirit world. This odd way of thinking about time and spirit communication was present as I thought about the events of the seance at the Royal Oak. Speaking with my more spiritual friends within the paranormal community had given me the incentive, so to speak, to learn more. However, it is not all that simple, as whilst some aspects make sense, others do not and that leaves me in a position of disbelief; something which can make a spiritual journey a little short.

At one point following the seance at the Royal Oak, I even attempted to discover more by visiting a spiritual church near my home in Hertfordshire; however, I found myself unable to enter due to feeling that the energy of the place felt unbalanced. That in itself is odd. In fact, I attempted it a few times only to be presented with the same result.

I have also been connecting with other mediums too, a couple of which have been a great help providing advice over Facebook. All of which are encouraging me to follow this spiritual path now open to me. Many of them even understand my confusion and reluctance to move forward with it. Oddly, the journal that I have always used to document the events of paranormal investigations, general paranormal research and even sketch out article ideas was suggested to be used to document my spiritual journey.

The mediums all advised that once I had updated my journal and begun to understand my journey into the spiritual side that the next stage was to find a good meditation technique that worked for me. When I can successfully meditate, I should be able to converse with my spirit guides more easily. However, this is where my spiritual journey towards potential mediumship came to an abrupt end. You see, for some reason, I am not someone who can easily meditate; in fact, I find it near on impossible. When someone says to "clear your mind" I usually respond with "how?" which seems to totally confuse them, as usually people just do it. I researched many different meditation techniques to try to achieve a meditative state of mind, but none worked. I wondered if this was due to my mind always being busy and full of ideas, questions and more, or if it was connected with my epilepsy. Either way, meditation was looking to be out of reach, and meeting my own personal spirit guides even further out of reach.

With my own potential spirit journey coming to an abrupt end, which was more of an end before it even got started, I knew I would have to rely on the information provided by others who were somewhat more sensitive than I clearly was. However, this provided me with a new way of investigating the paranormal, which had been there all along but now was more obvious and relevant to me, involving mediums to provide information they pick up on a location to help add to an investigation. I think many people make the mistake of being led by the medium so that they forget to remain objective and end up investigating subjective elements that do not have a factual bearing on a case. I did not want to do that, especially for the Royal Oak case. However, I wanted to be accepting of the role spirituality plays in the case and involve it in the process moving forwards, hopefully to benefit the result.

The return to the Royal Oak in June, 2013, and the seance that we conducted was potentially a game changer as far as the case would state. It had left me with some very strange experiences, which I had little explanation for, to be honest, but knew I needed to know more about. I also felt that I needed to incorporate more spirituality into the investigation. This also highlighted to me that the locals and, in particular, Rachael's own spiritual circle were equally important when it came to understanding what was occurring at the Royal Oak. An important addition being how strangers would be drawn to the little old pub only to find they would either discover their spiritual abilities there or if they already knew their abilities, they would find welcoming new friends. It was certainly evident at this stage that spirituality and potentially past lives were very much becoming a part of the main thread of this case. This intrigued me, as often at many locations the history of the place was often associated with the haunting, but when it came to the Royal Oak in Swanage, it seemed as if the present people that were locating themselves there had become entwined with those that lived there over one hundred years earlier. Whether this could be considered a past life situation or that they were simply channelling these past individuals, that remained to be understood.

In order to perhaps understand these strange connections better, we would have to take a trip and understand the story of those that were at the Royal Oak over one hundred years prior. The very individuals that Rachael and her circle believed were communicating through them and also possibly haunting the pub on a regular basis. For that though, we would need to start at another pub: the Ship Inn.

Chapter Four

A Ghost Story Within a Ghost Story

The winter of 1878 was particularly severe with England feeling the sharp hit of sub-zero temperatures on a regular basis. It was the kind of deep cold winter that just seemed to continue to test the country's ability to survive. As the weather showed no remorse, the residents of Langton Matravers began to feel more than just the cold, they felt a real struggle to survive.

Situated between the villages of Herston (now a part of Swanage) and Acton, but not too far from the coast in Dorset, in 1878 much of the village was probably reliant on the other businesses in the area. Apart from a few more affluent residents, it was likely the extended winter was beginning to cause some residents financial problems as their main source of income was hindered by the cold weather.

One such resident was John Ball, the landlord of the Ship Inn in the village at the time this harsh winter struck. As such, it is likely that business may have been slower than normal. This would have undoubtedly added to the man's stress at the time, but perhaps there was more to this story as what happened next has always been a part of the greater Royal Oak story that fascinated me.

Following the closing of the Ship Inn on the night of 18 December, 1878, John Ball and his wife, Mary, began to argue. It is evident, due to the outcome, that the argument must have severely escalated. There are several stories that have been presented to me as I have researched this odd connection. The first being that following the argument Mary went upstairs to bed, however, she heard some commotion downstairs, so headed down to investigate. It is said that she was confronted with her husband preparing to take his own life with a shotgun; on seeing her, he decided that he would take her life too. This signified the beginning of a chase where Mary ran back upstairs and climbed out of the window, dropping to the ground below. John pursued her still, shotgun in hand, so she headed across to her mother's house which was in close proximity. As Mary barely closed the front door of her mother's house behind her, it was hit as John discharged the shotgun towards her. As he was unsuccessful in taking his wife's life, he returned to the Ship Inn, sat down in the public room and shot himself.

There have been some variations of this particular story that I have heard now, such as that, initially, he was trying to hang himself. When Mary discovered this, she ran out of the pub whilst he made chase with the shotgun from behind the bar. With regard to the argument itself, that often takes on various forms too. Some versions place the blame on Mary, postulating that she was having an affair and when John discovered this, he felt he could live no longer so decided to take her life and his. There is also the view that perhaps as John was failing to make a success of the Ship Inn, he could no longer live with this failure and decided to take his life. Perhaps originally he felt this would free Mary and allow her to have a better life without him, or perhaps he always intended to kill her too.

Domestic murder-suicide is a complex act, even today little is truly understood of the exact motive for each particular case; especially as in most cases those who could have explained are those who are dead. However, an online article posted in October, 2022, on the LEB website, https://leb.fbi.gov/articles/featured-articles/domestic-murder-suicide-a-compound-tragedy, provides the following potential motives for murder-suicide.

- Significant negative dynamic, such as abuse, infidelity, or perceived injustice, that exists in the relationship between the assailant and victim.
- Perpetrator's feeling of obligation toward the victim, such as protecting spouse, partner, or child from the stigma or shame of the planned suicide or the hurtful consequences of something the actor has done.
- Assailant's sense of mercy to relieve the victim of ongoing suffering or indignity because of illness or disability.

Whilst we only have limited information available to us with regard to the case related to John Ball, we could make some informed decisions based on these motives. I do not believe that John's decision to take his own life was based around an illness or disability; and as such relieving Mary of the ongoing suffering related to this potentially. However, it may be worth holding onto this thought a little, as it may be relevant later in the story of Mary Ball.

The second motive is highly possible in this instance, but I actually struggle to align with this one personally. Although I cannot prove or disprove that the second motive is right or wrong, it just does not sit correctly with me with regard to this and the wider story.

This leaves us with the first motive and brings us back to the possibility of two potentials: Infidelity, which could be on either part, to be fair. Whilst it is obvious perhaps to suggest Mary, John could have equally been at fault here and not been able to live with the guilt. There is also the possibility of abuse too, but again we have no evidence to support this.

Murder-suicide is a rare occurrence today, even though the media provides the perception that they are common crimes. In fact, according to the National Confidential Inquiry into Suicide and Safety in Mental Health, an approximate sixteen cases per year in England and Wales are recorded, even though there are thousands of suicides reported.

Whether John intended to only kill himself and things got out of hand, or his plan was always to kill Mary, the events that took place on that cold December night in 1878 sparked more changes than John Ball could ever imagine. They would change the course of Mary's life forever, the Ship Inn as it was then would be no more, and in death John would help make changes that would benefit others that would commit suicide in the future.

As John Ball had committed suicide in 1878, he would not be allowed to be buried on consecrated ground, as this was the law of the time. Instead, he was taken outside the village and was to be "buried like a dog" in a random field in an unmarked grave. This was because the act of suicide was seen as a criminal act upon oneself; as such the perpetrators were seen as committing a double criminal act. Firstly, it was seen as a spiritual offence in that it was against the wishes of God. Secondly, it was seen within the eighteenth-century school of thought that those that would commit suicide had homicidal tendencies. In John Ball's case this could be argued to be true. This also leads to other possibilities such as the bodies of those who commit suicide, like John, requiring burial at night with no service, or burial at crossroads with a stake driven through their hearts. It was believed that those who could commit such an act as suicide would have malevolent souls, so they would be buried away from the community in a manner that would protect the community. Superstition was clearly a big thing in Victorian times. If memory serves me well, the location of a crossroads was to confuse the spirit if it did rise, but the stake through the heart should prevent that from occurring. Those of you with an attention to detail would have most likely made the quick connection to Bram Stoker's Dracula. Oddly, this practice of a stake through the heart is not restricted to England. I have heard of its use in Romania when I visited Bran Castle there, which is not Dracula's castle but certainly a potential inspiration of Stoker's.

However, in this case it certainly seems as if John Ball was simply buried in a field outside the village and not on a crossroads. Whether a stake was driven through the man's heart or not, remains something that will only be known to those that buried him.

At the time, the local rector found the treatment of the local man completely unreasonable and called for the law to be reformed. It is said that it was this that began the change to allow those that committed suicide to be buried on consecrated ground, but I am not entirely sure it was this one event that changed this law. Certainly, there were changes to the law after John's suicide that meant burial on consecrated ground was allowed, but it is also apparent that such changes to the law were well underway prior to his death. So, perhaps whilst John Ball's suicide was not the catalyst for this change in the law, it was certainly a contributing factor. Something which made his death significant in helping to change the future, regardless of his motive for such an act.

The story of the Royal Oak and its possible haunting has evolved continuously since my first visit back in 2010, but that evolution certainly did not begin with me or my involvement with the pub. One question an investigator should always ask is when this began. This simple question often helps to initiate dialogue around experiences that someone may have encountered. In my own experience the answer to this usually takes on two clear aspects: the first being that their experiences began at a certain point in time within the property that they now live in and believe to be haunted, hence my involvement; the second being that their experiences started many years ago and are not related specifically to one location. This can provide a potential understanding of how we may be dealing with either a haunted property or possibly a haunted person. Neither are really that simple to confirm, let alone prove. For example, it could be said that an individual is not so much haunted as potentially gifted from a psi perspective.

As we have already heard, Rachael's encounters with paranormal activity started not long after she took on the place as its new landlady. However, we quickly discovered that this experience and the many that followed, were not simply the beginning. Rachael has also shared the slightly more vague recollection of a brief experience she had back in the 1980s when she worked at the pub. Oddly at that point she mentioned nothing of activity being experienced on the ground floor, but during the one time that she ventured upstairs, she would encounter something that simply left a dislike for the upstairs of the building. This feeling must have had a true impact on the younger Rachael, as she then refused to go upstairs again. In fact, this would remain until she became the pub's landlady and would have to overcome this fear.

When we discussed this earlier in the book it was from notes in my journal that had me thinking that this was something I refer to as a potential "alpha case", a term I learnt from my friend Greg Lawson in his book, *Detecting Paranormal.* Whilst I always liked the concept of the alpha case, a case in which the first report of paranormal activity may influence following cases, I equally recognised the approach from my history studies in the past. In order to fully understand the case, we need to investigate. We often seek out additional sources to help support the possibility of paranormal activity. Most often these come in the format of witness testimony, which recounts the experiences of others at the same location. The more witnesses the better, and the more witnesses that have had no interaction but recall similar encounters, are better still.

However, Lawson's "alpha case", or the primary source, is always important to a case as that can help define the potential origins of a haunting. Origins which could be seen to be paranormal or equally likely have a completely normal explanation. As investigators we must take into consideration at all times that there is always the potential for a completely logical explanation to paranormal activity that has been lost somewhere along the way, leaving a dramatic haunting and often a bloody good ghost story.

Researching more into the history of the Royal Oak also inspired my interest in finding the primary source or at least trying to. After all when it comes to the investigation of hauntings, it is not easy to seek out the primary source. This is due to the simple fact that more often than not these cases begin as simple ghost stories, perhaps shared between only a few people. We can only really find our way back to the originally documented instance. An instance which may be the result of decades of ghost stories being shared until someone wishes to lay them down in print.

In 2013, David Leadbetter did exactly this in his book *Paranormal Purbeck – A Study of the Unexplained* providing some of the Royal Oak's ghostly stories in print for all to read. It has also assisted in providing a couple of accounts that help us begin to build a timeline of encounters and our journey towards the primary source. The only problem is that these accounts are currently no more than secondary sources, accounts documented and presented by Leadbetter himself.

There is, of course, one other place that a few strange encounters were documented and that is on social media, the same posts that I originally read prior to my own visit to the Royal Oak. We covered some of these in Chapter Two, however, they did not really appear to provide much of a timeline, apart from one which mentions the year 2009.

The first odd experience documented by Leadbetter in his book occurred back in 2007 to one Mark Elford. What is particularly interesting about this first oddity is that it touches on one of the more interesting phenomena at the Royal Oak: that of time slips. Whilst the term may sound like something out of a science fiction novel, the basics of it are that those who experience them find themselves in a time which is no longer their own.

As I have never experienced this personally, I had to do a little research into this strange phenomenon, and one location in the UK which appeared to be top of the list for its relationship with time slips appeared to be Bold Street in Liverpool. This mind-boggling urban legend certainly captures your imagination but would have greater meaning later in the story of the Royal Oak. The Bold Street time slip appears to have been encountered by more than one individual over the years, which helps us to understand the possibility that they can occur more than once in one location, again, essential to the Royal Oak story. Some that have encountered the Bold Street time slip have stated that they have been transported back to Victorian times, whilst others have travelled to the more recent 1950s or 1960s. Witnesses to this odd phenomenon have encountered all kinds of things from other times such as vehicles, period clothing and changed surroundings. The experience itself obviously leaves people somewhat disorientated, feeling strange and then becoming aware that their surroundings have changed. What is even more odd is that some people have stated that they have interacted with people from the other times. However, the people they meet are not obviously troubled by their strange modern appearance. After a little time has passed, their surroundings return to their present time. Such stories remain based only on the personal accounts captured and are the stuff of urban legend with no clear solid scientific proof to back them up.

Still in 1996, a former police officer called Neil Rose was said to have a strange experience in Bold Street. As he walked towards a bookstore, he found himself in a street with people dressed in 1950s fashions and cars from the same era parked on the road. A clothes shop had replaced the bookstore he was heading towards. Oddly he also bumped into a woman who was also dressed in modern clothes, she appeared to be equally confused by the situation. Many other stories of time slips have been provided for other locations, making it an interesting phenomenon.

Mark Elford's 2007 time slip experience, according to Leadbetter, occurred during a game of pool in the back room near the cellar. As he headed towards the door close to the cellar to collect a ball that had escaped the table, Elford became aware that he was outside, even though he was not. He believed that he experienced a displacement of time, which had him feel as if he was in the backyard in another time. In his account he described himself as being invisible or at least that there was nothing physically of him there in that time. Elford mentioned to Leadbetter the year 1710 in relation to this experience, but was unclear why he did so.

Four to six years prior to his time slip experience in the back bar, Mark Elford also provided Leadbetter with another experience. This was of an apparitional sighting similar to that which has been provided by others I have spoken to over the year. Elford, on this occasion, saw a woman behind the bar, situated in the right-hand corner. He advised Leadbetter that this apparition was dressed in a gown and an old-fashioned cap that he associated with Victorian fashion. He would also provide an encounter with the same woman to Leadbetter that occurred closer to 2011, but as this appears to be more spiritual in its nature and clearly not helping with the search of the primary source, I won't include it here.

At this point, Elford's experiences documented by Leadbetter takes our timeline of activity all the way back to the year 2001. A year which has always been difficult to forget for many of us the world over. It was a year that both began and ended in tragedy. On 26 January, 2001, an earthquake measuring 7.9 on the Richter scale hit Gujarat, India, killing an estimated 20,000 people and possibly injuring 167,000. The devastation was unimaginable and India's strongest earthquake since the 1950s. During the summer months here in the UK, two airlines were hijacked and flown into the twin towers of the World Trade Center in New York. The collapse of the towers caused widespread damage and 3,200 people were killed or missing due to those attacks. A third plane crashed into the Pentagon in Washington D.C.

Our memories of events can be odd at the best of times, but I wonder if you remember both of those events taking place in 2001. Equally odd would be the activity at the Royal Oak, which would continue to reach back further that 2001 when it's previous landlady, Sharan, would tell me about her encounters at the pub in the year 2000.

As I covered in Chapter Two, Sharan was a former landlady at the Royal Oak long before Rachael took over as its current landlady. Sharan provided some really interesting accounts of paranormal activity during her stay at the pub. All of which lend themselves to the accounts which would follow that could provide us with a good candidate for our primary source. Firstly, Sharan, too, encountered time slips like Mark Elford, but hers occurred in the top floor bedroom known as the twin bedroom. Looking out of the window, she would sometimes see orchards rather than the houses that should be seen. Oddly, a vision that one of the ladies attending the Victorian seance in the future would see from the other bedroom on that floor, providing us with multiple instances of time slips throughout the building, potentially.

Sharan also provided accounts of apparitions, audible phenomena and objects moving by themselves, all of which would be encountered by others after her time at the Royal Oak. To date, Sharan's account of her family's time at the pub provides the most detailed indication of varied phenomena which would be encountered in the future by others either living there or visiting.

However, Leadbetter came through once again finding another excellent witness that would predate even Sharan. Jsanine Jenkins lived at the Royal Oak for about 16 months from early 1998. At this point her mother, Christine, was running the pub. Jsanine advised Leadbetter in her 2011 interview with him that she had encountered activity only a couple of months after they had moved in. The description given appears to tell of a levitating Guinness glass, which raised from the counter and later smashed on the floor. This occurred in the earlier months of 1998. In June of the same year, Jsanine told Leadbetter about their cat acting oddly, which was also something that Sharan had advised me of during her family's time at the pub. Loud, heavy footsteps, similar to that of workmen's heavy boots were heard on the landing by Jsanine. Again, a phenomenon that has been repeatedly reported over the years at the pub. Just two months later, Jsanine recalled footsteps being heard again upstairs, but this time it sounded like running and was heard by more than one person. Oddly, Jsanine also recounts that the previous landlord asked if they had heard the "landing walker", indicating the distinct possibility that this activity may still predate Jsanine's time at the pub too.

As investigators of the paranormal we are often restricted by the information we receive, some locations may only yield one or two witnesses, whilst others may provide us with numerous to consider. The Royal Oak has always been an intriguing location for me, as the witnesses just seem to continue to present themselves in one way or another. Time, it would seem, was always a little strange with our familiar understanding of its linear presentation being somewhat elusive. Even our witnesses had been impacted by this with some of them coming forward in the future to tell us about their past experiences, or sometimes having experiences between our visits. While I researched the timeline backwards to seek out the primary source, it would be reaching out into the future from the present day, growing its reach, often making me wonder if there would ever be an end to this particular case.

Although I am almost certain that there may be additional experiences of the paranormal at the Royal Oak that pre-date Rachael's late 1980s interaction with the location, I am unable at the time of writing this book to source witness statements to support this assumption. Through my time at the pub speaking to those present there, it would certainly not surprise me if there had been reports of paranormal activity dating back to those we thought were interacting with us during the sittings that we had over the years. More on that strange possibility later, though, perhaps.

As investigators of the paranormal we must concentrate on what we can prove, what we have as evidence to support the case we are investigating. In the absence of such evidence, we must focus on what we have available. In the case of the Royal Oak, it almost appears as if the primary source of its haunting may in some weird twist be related to Rachael herself, her younger self, at that point in the late 1980s when she ventured upstairs only to be met with an experience that prevented her from returning to the first floor until she had become the pub's landlady.

Once again the concept of time comes to mind. Is it possible that Rachael's initial interaction was somehow connected to her future at the pub? Perhaps, as I think Rachael believes, it was connected to the pub's past at a time in the late 1800s when the Stevens family were involved with the pub. Of course, there is also the distinct possibility that Rachael's initial experience is a false memory; as investigators we must consider all possibilities in a case such as this one. It may be that Rachael has misremembered experiences that she believed to be factual. The key here being the term "believed" as this acknowledges that the witness truly believes that they had experiences, however, the finer details could be slightly mixed up. Sometimes this can mean a perfectly normal experience with a completely logical explanation can be confused with a strange experience.

The odd thing is that whilst actively investigating the case of the Royal Oak, I never really asked Rachael if she had previous experiences at the Royal Oak that would pre-date her taking over as its landlady. The focus for us and her remained on her experiences whilst she was currently there. We gathered witness statements from the previous landlady and those that were having experiences during our time there, but exploring the primary sources got lost in the noise of current activity. Something which has taught me a valuable lesson in my own approaches to investigation. Does understanding that potentially the primary source of the Royal Oak case could be Rachael change anything? I do not think so, if anything it provides an interesting dynamic to the case that I have not really encountered before. Remember, between Rachael having her first odd experience in the late 1980s until I got involved in 2019 that there had been numerous individuals that had their own experiences completely detached from Rachael's. Equally her initial experience differed greatly from more recent ones, but some of those between had similarities to later experiences. All of which suggest a possibility of the activity evolving over time at the Royal Oak.

Is it possible, I wonder, if Rachael being sensitive to spirit was something that helped trigger this activity, which then evolved over time to the level we have seen in the past? Then in a strange ironic turn, Rachael herself took over the pub to manage it, when really she was to manage a strange connection to the phenomena that she herself had triggered. It is a possibility we could consider, but as many things in the paranormal, not one we could easily prove or for that matter prove without difficulty. Again, as investigators we must adopt some logical thinking and in the absence of evidence, we have to chalk this particular point up to coincidence. Even as I type, I can hear Rachael disagreeing and rolling her eyes; when it comes to the Royal Oak, there have been a few occasions when I have believed something to be a coincidence only to be presented with more of the same to the point where it became a synchronicity. There have been a good few events at the Oak which have seemed coincidental but seemingly connected although lacking a reasonable causal explanation. So, until some additionally related events come to light, this one is coincidence, even if I am already questioning it myself.

Chapter Five

Table Design Seance

It is odd, really, as one thing I have learnt over the years is that there is importance in what occurs prior to an investigation and not just during the event itself. This is often missed by many ghost hunting groups and even seasoned investigators as the focus becomes the place at the time they are there. We still have little knowledge when it comes to understanding the paranormal, so restricting ourselves by things like time and space, seems to me like it could be an error we should not make. I have been reminded of this whilst reading about the concept of remote viewing, where individuals can utilise paranormal abilities to describe locations they are not present at, and from great distances away. If like me, my dad and my wife, Jen, you are a bit of a fan of the television series *Stargate*, then you may be surprised to learn that the American government ran a project with the same name for many years that investigated the value in remote viewing, by all accounts with great success. So, being present at a location does not necessarily define a better connection, we must allow ourselves to see beyond the conventional means of gaining knowledge, especially if we are to investigate the paranormal.

I make entries in my journal prior to investigations that outline my thoughts and ideas for upcoming visits to the Royal Oak, but equally, on occasion, when there seems to be a little more that comes to light whilst I am away from the pub. I thought it important to include some of this to help with the understanding of the bigger picture of this case. After all, many investigations at this strange little pub would leave me with more questions than answers, questions that I would have to discuss in order to gain an understand of them. If anything, certainly the paranormal generates a wealth of discussion and that, I feel, is a massive positive for this interesting yet sometimes confusing subject.

It was Thursday, 4 July, 2013, American Independence Day, something which I would gain much more understanding of when I would visit the States in 2023 with my family. As my American friends celebrated their independence, I rang my mum to update her about my paranormal journey, which by all accounts at that time was leaning more and more towards the spiritual. At the time, I had been experimenting with forms of meditation to attempt to understand how the mediums I was getting to know may be able to place themselves in such a dissociative state, allowing spirits to potentially speak through them. In order to achieve this, I needed a "place" to focus on and calm my mind. Whilst the usual meadows and such had failed miserably, a walk in Astonbury Woods, near to the town where I lived, provided this calming effect in reality, so perhaps it might do the same during meditation.

My mum totally understood this, as it was a place where she too had felt peace when visiting. She used to care for the wood by doing regular conservation work there and on the odd weekend, I had gone with her to help. In fact, I recall clearing areas of the wood with her and having our coffee breaks whilst sat on logs. In England, our local wooded areas are fading fast to make way for more roads or more housing, but this little piece of wood has managed to survive a few times in the past. Recently, this occurred again, with housing threatening its existence, individuals were called to action and once again my mum and I provided our support to save the wood.

Talking to my mum about the wood, she mentioned that there was a possible ancient road that passed through it, which could equally help provide reason for our connection to this place. However, I thought the connection for me was more to do with family, and with this in mind I asked if my grandfather (the pocket watch one) had been to the wood, as I had oddly felt him there. She confirmed that he had been on several occasions and helped look after the wood as we had; that is three generations of our family ensuring that Astonbury Wood was well kept, giving our time and thought to its preservation. Mum also added that there was something else too: when my grandfather sadly passed away, she placed some of his things in the woods. This was something I knew nothing of but actually made perfect sense to me.

I know that usually, as far as I understand it, a medium creates a place in their mind that they visualise as a part of their meditation to help connect with spirits. However, that was certainly something that I struggled greatly with over the years, but utilising Astonbury Woods, a real place, actually worked really well. I always thought it was quite odd how the place was so close to my home and so accessible for me. This was made very apparent during a "life event" that left me feeling both angry and upset. I blindly headed to the woods alone. At the time I was not even sure why I went there, but once there and walking through them, I encountered shards of light penetrating the canopy at random points, many different types of wildlife, but beyond all this natural beauty, I found an overwhelming sense of calm. The woods that I had known since childhood, which three generations of my family had cared for, and where items of my grandfather's now lay, now looked after me. I have to believe that there is a greater story in that alone. It certainly made me aware that perhaps I needed to be open minded to the spiritual approaches I was encountering at the Royal Oak; certainly the connection to my grandfather demanded it.

On Tuesday, 9 July, 2013, I wrote in my journal "returning to the Royal Oak in Swanage is something I now know I have to do".

I knew that we needed to attempt another seance and attempt communication across the three timelines. However, I did not wish to forget my roots within the paranormal. My previous visit to the Royal Oak had been all about connecting to the individuals and experiencing the events of that seance. This time around it would have to be more about setting it up with the aim to capture the events and understand it better. This still meant concentrating on the seance in the dining room, but this time I wanted to have a second team of more science and technology minded individuals monitoring the events of the night. They could also investigate the rest of the pub whilst the seance was in progress to understand if activity occurred elsewhere at this time. The idea was to cover as much as we could in order to try and understand what was truly going on.

In order to achieve this two-pronged attack, I enlisted the help of my new friend Graham Smith and his team. Smith's team would not have access to the seance room but would investigate the rest of the property. They would also need to time code the entire night to ensure that we can connect the dots between any events that may occur within the seance room and the rest of the pub. At lease that was the plan in July that I was working on.

On this occasion I wanted to try and change the approach of the seance a little by utilising my own approach and a visualisation of Astonbury Woods. Oddly. I thought this may unite the group together and possibly provide some interesting results. This was only a gut feeling, though, it had no real reason behind it and certainly no supportive evidence or data.

In preparation for my next investigation of the Royal Oak, I wanted to try meditation using Astonbury Woods as a focal point; on Wednesday, 10 July, 2013, I decided to give it a go and document in my journal what had occurred. Whilst a part of the process according to my more spiritual friends was to connect with one's spirit guides, I am not sure whether or not I was ready to believe they existed at that point and perhaps that hindered the results somewhat.

I settled myself in a darkened room, there were two candles burning, but this was more by accident than design. In my left hand I held my own pocket watch, so that I could hear it ticking. In my right hand I held my grandfather's pocket watch. I then began to imagine myself entering the woods (based, of course, on the aforementioned Astonbury Woods) and then walking through the dark enclosed wood, with only shafts of light piercing through the canopy from time to time. As I walk through the wood connecting with nature, I also discard my own worries and thoughts, clearing my mind. When I encounter difficulty, I try to clear things from my mind; I imagine that I am once again clearing parts of the wood, helping to care for it. Once this is achieved, I find a clearing, which is illuminated by blinding light. As I step into the circular clearing, I am blinded briefly by this light, but it also makes me feel warm and protected. My vision gradually returns, allowing me to see more of the clearing, at the same time I feel more and more protected. At the centre of this circle is a gigantic oak tree with solid roots that head deep underground and branches that reach high into the heavens. I walk into the centre of the clearing and place the palm of my hand on the thick bark of the tree. At that point a great energy rises from the earth's core, flows through the oak's roots and up the tree into me, grounding me naturally. I then ask out loud, if, with the greatest respect, I could connect with my own spirit guides.

Whilst I was not really sure what exactly I was expecting at this point in the meditation, I know that perhaps I was hoping for a sign to confirm that my grandfather was my spirit guide. As far as I am aware, this did not happen. I do have to admit that I was not sure if I had rushed it all a bit! However, as I lay there on that Wednesday night, attempting to connect with my spirit guides, some oddities did occur. At one point I did feel slightly cold and even shivered at times. I saw a face in my head, but I did not recognise it at all. It was also in black and white, and the name Roger came to mind, which also meant little to me.

On that same evening I also tried to use my own pocket watch as a pendulum, asking if my grandfather was present. The watch moved ever so slightly. I asked if he was my spirit guide, the watch moved a slight amount again. Still nothing conclusive though. Nothing I received was enough to be a firm response. I ended this meditation by thanking the spirits for their help as I had read about and seen in action at the Royal Oak.

Although a little disappointed with my first adventure in spiritual meditation, my more spiritual friends did say it was something that you have better results with the more you practise. My thoughts were drawn to the process based on what I had read about over the years. I felt that my approach required more structure perhaps.

The next day I spoke to Rachael, which was a little odd, to be fair, as it was like speaking to a close family member and we spoke for over an hour without really stopping. Rachael informed me that the pub was still very active and it would appear that her spiritual circle was having good results connecting with spirit. Roy, especially, was coming along a little, but perhaps becoming a little out of control at times. This was something Rachael was becoming increasingly concerned about. She advised that it would appear as if Roy was connecting with spirits related to the local area and also making a reference to Bernadette. She was concerned that Roy appeared to be on a similar path to Andrew, but Roy seemed to be linked to the past, whilst Andrew was linked to the future. A strange statement in itself.

Rachael and I continued to talk, and I advised her of my plans for the next visit and investigation, which would be on Saturday, 31 August, 2013. I explained my plan for a seance, and also the involvement of Smith's team to investigate elsewhere.

It was very much about beginning to document these personal experiences, to build a timeline, but also to capture any other evidence we may find too.

I mentioned to Rachael my recent attempts to meditate and she advised me that her original meditation had been something she also found quite hard to do originally. She advised that she does not really find time to meditate but still manages to connect with spirits. Sometimes you have to find what works for you as an individual, meditation may not be a part of that, whilst for some it may be essential. I advised that there were certain places that I was beginning to find myself more connected to such as Astonbury Woods and even the Royal Oak. When I was physically present in these places, the connection was different, they changed my emotional state and sometimes cluttered my busy mind.

On Friday, 9 August, 2013, less than a month before the next investigation at the Royal Oak, I headed to Milton Keynes to meet up with Graham Smith and his team-mate Matt. I wanted to work with Smith's team, RSVP UK, as they showed similar approaches to my own; Smith displayed that certain passion that a select few within the paranormal community display. It was for those reasons that I knew he was the right person to work with on the Royal Oak case. What I did not know was that the chance meeting at Bradwell Abbey was actually the beginning of many collaborations, and that our friendship would keep us in contact for many years to come. In fact, Bradwell Abbey would become another long-term investigation and a place he would have experiences, but also test out theories and technology of his own. It was also the location where we would conduct a series of seances in a crude attempt to recreate the Scole Experiment. Although, that is another story, for another time.

As I spoke to Graham and Matt on that Friday evening, I soon understood that they were as equally detailed as I was with my investigations. At the time their client report, in my opinion, was presented better than my own. It was also apparent that they liked to present themselves as professional and serious investigators researching the paranormal, rather than a group simply out for an experience of a paranormal nature over the weekend. At that time my only worry was that Smith and his team would come across too focussed on the science and their search for evidence. This is actually great, but in my experience an approach like that can often lead to the creation of conclusions based on what the client tells us alone. It can also mean you can wrongly evaluate the client during those initial meetings. I know this simply because I have made this mistake myself, but these days I take on board the client's story and experiences, then add them to the wider understanding of the case as a whole. After all it is these stories of ghostly experiences that become the basis of most paranormal investigations. So, these days I tend to work using the stories as a foundation to build upon. To these, we add more experiences and stories, any supporting evidence we may record. Understanding where these may intersect and support each other often helps to provide the bigger picture of the case itself. As someone with a keen interest in history and simply because I have seen the history of a location play a part in many cases, I also tend to look into the history of a case too, whether that's the location's history, a person's history or both. Similar to a criminal case, a paranormal case needs to be built and constructed to provide enough information to support the belief, for want of a better term. As investigators it is this gathering of information that we focus on, but sadly these days I see few people that still take the time to ensure this is done. Instead, we often see their experiences dramatically displayed on YouTube, with little or no evidence in reality.

I left my meeting with Smith feeling confident that we were on the same page, he understood my need to capture good evidence but equally remain open to the spiritual side to gain understanding of that side of things too. Smith's logic and reminders would continue to keep me focussed over the years as we worked together, challenging each other at every turn. Some may have even seen us as a bit of a double act from time to time, there were certainly a couple of paranormal conventions where that was the case.

On Monday, 19 August, 2013, I wrote an entry in my journal that began, "Quite a bit has occurred now! Things are beginning to fall into place for 31 August." These were confusing times for me as I continued to try and understand more of the spiritual side of this case. Sometimes it felt a little like I was allowing myself to accept things that were more fantasy than fact, but luckily that was where Smith would continue to help keep me on the straight and narrow.

At that point in time, I had received word from a psychic medium called Stewart Keeys who I had been in communication with through Facebook. He had made arrangements to also visit the Royal Oak on 31 August for a few hours. His intent was to look at the Royal Oak as a location for his paranormal web-series. However, I think at that point, through our discussions online, that Keeys was beginning to see a greater potential for the pub.

With all this in mind, I shared with Keeys a strange design that I had received on the way home. He had called it a "spirit communication platform, like I've never seen before". He also commented on compass directions, but there was no compass on the version I had sent him. Those directions were the cardinals North, East, South and West. Oddly, I saw this as a potential understanding that the design's directional position was important too, which would need to be understood. It was lucky that I had recently acquired a compass!

I was still left wondering if the design had real meaning and even potential use, or was it simply something my imagination had put together in a tired state after a strange night at the Royal Oak. With others seemingly placing importance in it,

I felt it certainly could not be ignored. As such it would be used to the best of my understanding, but knowing Rachael was not keen on the use of objects like Ouija boards within the pub, I had to wonder if she would adopt its use at all.

As the investigation fast approached, the position of the table played on my mind a lot. Referring to something Gina had said whilst in trance last time, I began to wonder if it had a relationship to the sun and potentially the moon. Elemental symbolism also began to come to light during this thought process too, and I started to look at alchemical and older symbols for the four elements, Fire, Water, Earth and Air. This kind of symbolism is not a huge surprise as Rachael had on occasion mentioned that she believed that Bernadette may have been a witch of some sort. Equally, Rachael had also mentioned around this time that the infinity symbol had been seen a few times too, a symbol which could be related to magic and represent equilibrium or balance of various forces. Obviously, in more modern times it has become a secular mathematical symbol for infinity in numbers, time or space. Past, present or both understandings seem to mean something here. Even Keeys was beginning to pick up on a few symbols related to the Royal Oak at this time, so perhaps utilising the design was without doubt the correct route to take.

Often, we talk about paranormal investigations beginning with the moment we set foot at the location. Whilst I have had numerous "feelings" when arriving at a location allowing me to ascertain if it may be a good active night or a potentially quiet night, it was not until I started to re-read my own journal entries that I began to realise the wealth of things that occur prior and post investigations. These include our odd realisations and thought processes, those strange conversations and our decisions to take a certain approach, the questions we may ask as we remain unsure of something, and the answers we may receive from others around us. That is not to mention those odd connections, those synchronicities that occur, especially when our minds are in that place of high strangeness.

A case becomes a part of us, true investigators, and as such our experiences reach beyond time and space of an investigation.

On Friday, 30 August, 2013, I think I got up really early and made my way to the Royal Oak, arriving around nine in the morning and missing any major traffic on the roads. At least that is what I believe I may have done, as I have nothing written in my journal to support these travel plans. Over the years, I have travelled down early morning to miss traffic on numerous times, so it is logical that this may have been the approach on that morning.

I spent the day working on a report for my day job but as the evening approached, the energy at the pub was clearly beginning to build. The quiet almost homely atmosphere of the bar area, which had been present throughout the day, now started to dissipate as the locals entered the premises and took up their usual places. As I watched from the side lines, I saw the theatre in these social interactions, the greetings, the usual drinks and the catch up of the week's events around town. One or two of them recognised me and greeted me like a local, welcoming me into their social dynamic. I felt present, accepted and acknowledge by the group.

Nick arrived during the early evening, but he was without his wife, Gina, and soon relaxed after a few drinks. He too was welcomed as a local, even though he did not reside in Swanage and lived a good couple of hours away. Again, this was telling of the welcoming atmosphere of this little Dorset pub; something which the pub itself seemed to generate, but so did its locals. The core group of which were accepting, welcoming and made you feel at home.

Following a late dinner with Nick and Rachael, I found myself in the Royal Oak's garden alone with Roy. The situation was odd to say the least, as I felt he wanted to know more about the paranormal, but for some strange reason I felt this was not wise at that time. Instead, we sat on a bench at the top of the garden close to the wall and discussed his life, pretty much right from the beginning. Roy has certainly had an interesting life and there are many experiences within it that would certainly make their own chapters, possibly even a book. However, that would be straying from the story at hand, the one of the Royal Oak.

An earlier conversation with Pete made me realise that we have our "tells" that indicate when spirits are close by and seek to interact with us. I am not entirely sure if I totally believe this, as I still struggle to believe if spirits or ghosts are specifically related to those that have passed away. I am not completely sold on the survival of death theory just yet, I guess that I still have a lot of research to do still. Plus, I am sure Smith would have something to say about me totally buying into the spiritual and get me back on track in no time.

The "tell" I spotted in Roy that evening was quite simple, he began to rub his arm. I had seen this previously and then the outburst in the twin room had occurred. Roy was beginning to do this during our conversation, so that is why I advised him to focus on telling his own life story, ensuring that what he spoke of was directly related to him and no other. It seemed to work.

Later Nick joined Roy and me in the garden, but quickly changed the conversation, mentioning Bernadette. A spirit that I was advised has been "cast out" of Roy by Terri during an eventful night at the Royal Oak, which I was not present for unfortunately. Nick seemed to believe that Bernadette was present in the garden with us at that point; this obviously distressed Roy.

We took the decision to head back inside the pub, where Roy's wife spoke to me about him. I think she was worried about potential spirits taking him over from time to time, and that he may have no control over this. Whilst I advised that I was most certainly no expert in these situations, perhaps one approach could be to try and focus Roy back on the here and now. Talking to him about things that are current and relevant, to stop him from focussing on other things that may be seen to be related to potential spirits looking to possess his body briefly.

As the night in the pub drew to a close, and the locals all headed off home slightly more lucid than they had arrived, Rachael closed up. Rachael, Nick and I continued to chat for a little while longer, and as Nick was a little more open to spirit due to alcohol, it was not long before one was communicating through him. This particular spirit was possibly French, called Henrich and apparently quite liked Champagne. After a little unrecognisable chat, an amazing balancing act, Nick dropped to the floor and the French spirit was gone. At this point he decided it was a good time to call it a night and headed up to bed. After a couple of words on the matter, Rachael and I followed him up to our respective rooms; mine was to be the Poppy Room on this occasion.

The morning came too soon and with it I was gifted a slight headache, which was probably due to the distinctive lack of sleep. So, I got up, headed downstairs and grabbed a few cups of coffee to get my day started. I would like to think I can function without coffee, but it does seem to be my go-to thing every single morning. Whilst on paranormal investigations, I probably drink a lot more than usual as I end up drinking it through the night rather than just at the normal morning interval.

It was now very much Saturday, 31 August, 2013, the day of the investigation. As I was already at the Royal Oak, I would likely have to guide a few new people there later that day to ensure their arrival. One such person was my cousin Clare Hinks and at around nine in the morning, she sent me a text message to advise that she was about to embark on the two and a half hour journey from her home in Cornwall to the Dorset pub. Prior to that day Clare had displayed certain mediumistic abilities whilst we were growing up; she certainly had travelled the more spiritual path in the world of the paranormal. I had always been sceptical of her abilities, but that's less a reflection on them and more something that highlights how I originally approached stranger phenomena. If anything, the Royal Oak case had already opened my mind to other possibilities, which I felt required exploration. Though Clare had, at that point, reduced her focus on her spiritual journey, as she had been focussed on being a mum to her children, that, I feel, was changing. So, I could not say if her journey to the Royal Oak that day would spark the return to the paranormal for her, or if she was already gradually returning anyway. Perhaps the events of that night were merely another push that she felt she could no longer ignore.

I spent my first couple of hours setting up the tables in the dining room and also speaking further with both Rachael and Nick. However, it was not long before Clare arrived at the Royal Oak. I met her outside, where she handed me the notes she had made prior to making the journey. This was based on the task I had set her of visualising a walk-through of the pub. She had done this, written it down and brought it with her, as instructed. This was based on an event when we were children, where Clare managed to describe the interior of my friend's house exactly right apart from two things, 1) the picture above the sofa was incorrect (I later discovered the one she described was present when my friend's grandfather was alive) and 2) her description of the house's interior seemed to have things like stairs in the wrong place (we later discovered the description was a mirror view of the property). So, with the success of this approach in the past, I thought perhaps this would be a good thing to try with the Royal Oak.

As we entered the pub together that morning, it was evident that Clare recognised the location from the exercise she had performed. She quickly began to point out things as we walked into the garden. I introduced her to Rachael and Nick, and we remained speaking to them for a little while. Then we headed upstairs, where I read through Clare's notes and we discussed my plans for the evening ahead. The notes she had made were pretty spot on by the way, which immediately helped to boost her confidence, as from this point forward she appeared to be picking up on things constantly. She even picked up on the presence of a curved wall on the first floor too.

Clare and I took a break from the pub and went for a walk. Although we did not make it to the location which Rachael had advised we visit, we did stop at a T-junction, which used to be a crossroads hundreds of years earlier and it was suggested that it could be the burial site of a suicide victim. At the time I did not realise the significance until I stumbled across it in *Paranormal Purbeck* by David Leadbetter. This would be one of those little pieces of the puzzle that may be important later, but then again it may not.

Shortly after this, we returned to the Royal Oak and things were beginning to gather momentum and people were also arriving bit by bit. Stewart Keeys arrived for his visit to the Royal Oak and spoke with us whilst he waited for his friend Alex. They were there to check the location over and measure it up for potential cables.

Stewart, Rachael and I did take some time to tour the pub and give Stewart an idea of the place. At this point Stewart remained "closed off" from the location and its spirits, not allowing them in, but I am sure he could feel the energy.

Ann and Dawn soon arrived and after a drink in the garden, I showed them upstairs. I also introduced them properly to Clare. The three began to help each other straight away. I felt Dawn was still a little closed off from the location, perhaps due to confidence as Ann was still teaching her. Later, Ann and Dawn attempted some pendulum work with good results. However, the mood dramatically changed in the room under Rachael's bedroom. Ann believed she could smell something really bad which frightened her too. This led them to close down and leave whatever it was well alone for then.

Next to arrive was Graham Smith and Matt from the RSVP UK Team. I had brought them in to conduct a more scientific investigation in the background, whilst a spiritual one was being conducted very much in the foreground. I believed this was for balance, but I am not really sure these days. I introduced them to Rachael and gave them a tour of the pub, which was difficult to achieve. I left them to set up their own investigation gear following a brief outline of the concept as it was in my head at that point in time. We then all simply waited for the go ahead from Rachael to begin, which meant waiting for Rachael to close up the pub so we could get started; something which appeared to occur earlier than first thought due to it being a quiet night at the Royal Oak.

As with previous investigations at the Royal Oak, we started with a walk around of the location, top to bottom. As one group, we headed to the twin room on the second floor. The guys from RSVP UK did not join us at this point, although I really wished they had now. I felt like I had alienated the more scientific side of the investigation. I knew it was something I would not do again.

Then as a group we settled into the twin room and some of the group began to pick up on things straight away. Nick started out in the rocking chair and almost straight away started to have feelings associated with his legs. I think at some point it may have even been said that he felt his legs were not there! Realising that this pain was a little much for him, Nick decided to get out of the chair. It was certainly at that point that someone, most likely Rachael, suggested that I sit in the chair.

Apprehensively, I took a seat and it felt strange. As I looked out into the room, I felt in control of the room. Oddly, I also felt everyone in there and at times a little of how they felt. As this occurred, Clare doubled over in pain, clutching her stomach; I realised that the energy was changing. It felt as if something else was there with us. At that point I am not exactly sure what I was doing, perhaps it was some kind of protection, or cleansing! To me it was what I should be doing. Perhaps it was returning the balance I believed was so important to the room and also setting boundaries. Although, I could not tell you why any of that came to mind and why I felt the need to act on it in that manner.

At this point Pete seemed to change! I could not see him at all; even though it was dark, you could make out faces, previously, but at this point I could only make out a silhouette of a man. Although Pete is quite tall and I was seated, this person was very large and well built. They appeared to turn in my direction, and it was as if they were squaring up to me. I felt like I should stand to take up this challenge but then decided against it for some reason. Whatever it was seemed to back off a little into the shadows and was gone. Both the feeling of its presence and its threatening silhouette disappeared into the darkness, leaving me somewhat confused. I tried to rationalise what I had experienced as simple shadow play in the room or perhaps members of the group, but in reality, it remained unexplained and plain odd.

Soon after this I made the suggestion to try the next room: the Poppy Room. As we stood in the Poppy Room, Clare picked up on quite a bit, but I was concerned about Ann. As we left the previous room Pete and Nick had also expressed their concerns for Ann too. I tried to gesture Dawn into helping Ann, but I do not think she understood what I was trying to communicate. However, oddly, Ann's protector spirit would soon make an appearance in order to help, it would seem. This was her grandfather, a large policeman. Oddly, once the spirit of her grandfather had been identified, Ann seemed much more like her usual self again.

This reminded me that my own family were prominent in my thoughts, including my own grandfather. In fact at different times, they had both been mentioned and connected to me, but with my sister and now cousin also being present at the Royal Oak, their presence almost felt natural. Oddly, I thought about Ann's description of her grandfather as her "protector" and I think my sister and cousin would have both attributed that kind of title to our grandfathers' spirits too. They were there if we needed them but equally they were a part of all this somehow. They obviously were not connected to the history of the Royal Oak but still felt connected to what we were trying to do there. It was emotional on various levels to be honest, but ultimately it was a nice feeling to know they may be there. Even for me, the family member that was a little more sceptical when it came to realising their presence.

We moved downstairs and into a slightly full room. This was the bedroom next to the kitchen. As we packed the entire group into this small space, Mo seemed to link in straight away. He gave us some information on a couple of the individuals, but then Rachael moved forward and his communicator seemed to recognise her and began to back off. The communicator indicated that some kind of violent abuse had taken place. Oddly, as Rachael decided to back off, I took the opportunity to move forward and received an interesting and profound message from Mo's communicator: "Communication is perception, perception is communication."

As confusing as this may sound, I have always thought that it made sense. The paranormal is a complex area of study that you must be open minded to when attempting to study it in full. Of course, you could approach it as a full-on sceptic and provide nothing but rational theories for all that goes on. Some of which would most likely be a good acceptable explanation. However, communication continues to be one of the most confusing elements of the paranormal. It is its source that provides that confusion too, as accepting that a spirit could be intelligently communicating with you would then mean you would have to accept the survival theory and that our spirits could survive bodily death. However, understanding that the communication could have different sources like our own minds or even the minds of others, provides completely different concepts. One being that of potential secondary personalities and the other presenting the possibility of supernormal powers capable of gathering information from the minds of others. The question still remains, how can we prove this either way? As an individual, your perception of communication defines how you see or understand what is going on during these paranormal events. So, this mirrored phrase meant quite a bit to me, to be fair, and resonated with my own understanding of what was possibly going on. However, we will return to this later in the book in order to discuss it in more depth and detail, with more of this fascinating story behind us.

Following this strange message, and as things began to calm, we decided to move further down the hallway to Rachael's rooms. We began by heading into the living room area where the CCTV hub was situated. However, as I stood by the door with Clare, Ann and Mo, I saw Nick speak with Rachael quietly. Instantly, I knew Nick was referring to Andrew as being in the room before us; he thought Andrew had been present in some kind of astral form as he was not there in person that night. As Rachael and Nick joined us, Ann seemed a little uncomfortable and mentioned a disgusting smell, which I could not smell. It was also around this time that Clare started to pick up on an energy of an angry spirit, possibly a man. She indicated he was not happy with the changes in the Royal Oak. She seemed to really connect with how he was feeling, so much so that at times I think she may have been channelling him.

We followed Clare into the next room, where she expressed her disgust at the new staircase. At times this was delivered to the group in such a manner that it came across a little comical to us all. This was good as it helped lift the mood of the group too. Although, I did feel for this spirit gentleman who was clearly not happy about Rachael's renovation work.

After a short amount of time Terri, Mo and I ascended the stairs to Rachael's bedroom area on the floor above. This was the same area where Pete and I had once sat amongst the dust, encouraging spirit to move my grandfather's pocket watch, only to receive a result that we were not really prepared for and one I have still not been able to debunk.

Straight away both Terri and Mo picked up on a few things in this space, but it was what Mo said that made the most sense. He mentioned something to do with the Church. Something I had commented on all day. In places, I thought the Royal Oak was a little like a church or a school. A place of belief, faith and learning. The other thing Mo mentioned was to do with being an explorer! Oddly this was something I had recently mentioned, as I had begun to see myself as an explorer of the paranormal and not just an investigator. This did not mean that I travelled the world, although that would be nice. I simply saw the paranormal and even the afterlife as an undiscovered country, and if all we were to learn was a part of a journey then surely making that journey to an undiscovered country was exploring. Equally as I tend to document my experiences and the experiences of others along the way, I felt this was a good description of what I did. Especially as the titles of ghost hunter and paranormal investigator were beginning to become blurred thanks to TV shows and the general community of the paranormal. Do not misunderstand me, I still saw myself as a paranormal investigator, but equally as a researcher and explorer. This was something that would later find its way to my website as I dropped the team approach and went out on my own. I wonder if it was Mo or indeed the spirits he was in communication with that evening that planted that seed and sent me off down a particular path. If so, then I thank them greatly.

We were then called back downstairs to the floor below, the first floor of the pub as Nick and Pete were now acting odd! We headed quickly down the staircase to find Pete asleep in the chair and Nick asleep under the stairs. At first, I thought they had simply fallen asleep waiting for us to return from the floor above; that was until Nick began to communicate. This time the communicator told us they were a small boy playing hide and seek in the hay loft. It was the strangest thing hearing this young boy's voice telling us about himself in what I can only describe as a childish mannerism, but all the while coming from Nick, a bigger well-built gentleman. It was like a poorly dubbed film, where the mouth movements do not match the language being spoken.

We talked Nick out of this by talking with the boy and asking him to back away from Nick. It appeared to be trance mediumship, but it was uncontrolled, perhaps more similar to possession. It occurred to me that we need better control of these situations. Oddly Nick came back, and Pete also woke up! Although I am unable to explain it, they both appear to be linked somehow.

Deciding that it was a good time to head to the bar area for a break and to prepare for the next part of our evening, we made our way back downstairs. Clare and I set up the dining room, leaving everyone else in the bar. At this point I asked everyone to look at pictures of the Stevens and Ball families, hoping that we could use this to help connect to them.

We pulled six of the rectangular dining room tables together to create one large table that we could sit around. I drew the strange design onto the tables in chalk; whilst it felt a little like I was drawing some magical design on the tables, no one really commented as such. In the central circle I wrote "1878" twice. I then placed three pocket watches on the table: my grandfather's,

Rachael's grandfather's and the large one with no hands. I also added Rachael's grandfather's compass as this had, oddly, turned up Thursday night. Rachael's mother and father had come in to see her at the pub as she thought she had located another pocket watch belonging to Rachael's grandfather. She handed it to Rachael who passed it onto me straight away. She instructed me to open it, which I did, but to my surprise it was not a pocket watch at all, it was a compass. Oddly, it was pretty similar to the one I had brought, brass in colour, with a cover that opens to reveal the directions. This was certainly odd.

I also ensured that there were plenty of pints of water placed around the table, as some of the locals appeared to require this once they returned from having a spirit communicate through them. I also wanted to see that if I placed something on the table that was not supposed to be there, whether or not it would remain.

With the room all set up and ready, I called everyone in, but looking back this is also where things went wrong!

Everyone apart from Nick entered the room, and I directed them to their seats. Nick was taking Storm, Rachael's dog, out into the garden, and consequently arrived at the table late. For me, how we all sat down seemed to be wrong, sort of disrespectful to what we were attempting to achieve.

Oddly for us all, the energy in the room seemed calm. I have to admit, I even felt a little as if this was the case too. It may be strange to comment on this, but as much of the approach here was of a spiritual nature, embracing the approach often meant that such things became more relevant. Perhaps it was due to being a part of a group where everyone was invested in this spiritual approach with many fully believing in the possibility that we were communicating with the departed personalities of those that may have once lived there. I asked Terri to begin the seance with a brief prayer, which she devised completely in the moment where it remains as my memory of it escapes me. Then

I advised the group that we did not need to touch the table, just focus our energy in order for it all to work! I was confident at the time that I knew what I was saying but looking back, I probably had little or no real idea. Energy was something I focussed on a great deal, expressing that it was key to these things being successful. In reality, I guess the term "energy" is vague in an explanation of odd occurrences. Perhaps I was simply buying into the moment or maybe just wishing it was as simple as it seemed to feel at that time. Either way, I felt like I knew what I was talking about, but in reality, I am not sure I did.

I looked up and around the table to check if everyone was alright with this strange approach, after all there was an odd design drawn on the tables in chalk, which could easily be mistaken for something out of a horror film. I could tell that some were apprehensive about the proceedings, which was understandable, but it was quite an honour that this group of people trusted my ideas in this and my approach.

Clare suggested that we all tried touching the table to make a connection, which seemed to make more sense to many present. I am also sure that this helped everyone to relax a little too, rather than being individuals around a table, they now felt more like a single collective group. It was shortly after this that Mo began to tap into something and pass information to the group. However, it was not related to the Royal Oak this time, it was more related to Clare and possibly my family. Something I was not expecting, to be honest.

Mo mentioned a little old lady who was hard of hearing and a little blind. We took this description to be a family member of ours called Aunty Elsie, my nan's sister. He then mentioned, what I heard as a dragon, but when I asked about it he corrected me telling me it was a dragonfly. These connect and possibly link to Peter, Elsie's son. Both were no longer with us. Mo then went on to describe a great trek to a mountain or something and that I would need a machete to get through the jungle. This was oddly significant to me as I have always wanted to visit Machu Picchu and had at that point done some research: getting there might have involved a trek through the jungle, machete in hand. These days it's a little easier to get there and less of a trek.

Mo then spoke to Clare providing her with some information regarding her spiritual path, mentioning a World War I letter, a drawer (second one down) and a bunch of soldiers she could see from her house window. Whilst strangely specific, nothing came to mind at the time or since. Perhaps, like many of these things, it may have a deeper spiritual meaning not yet understood. There again maybe not, it could just be random information with no relevance.

However, Mo also spoke at length about Clare's father, Nick, who died tragically in a flying accident when she was around two years old. It must have been both strange and emotional for Clare receiving such communication through Mo about someone she had lost when she was so young and unfortunately had little chance to really get to know. I am around a year or so older than my cousin, and I barely recall him either and that in itself is a little sad, I believe. I am fortunate to have had my father there for me throughout my life; he was an amazing father, and whilst he may have been tough on me at times, I am glad he was. I often think about lost connections of my own at times like these and wish I had done much better.

At this point Mo was completely different from what I had witnessed in the past, whilst not in trance at this point, he was certainly tuned in to something. Whilst he had connected to someone called Albert earlier on, potentially a local we were advised, there was still someone else present with Mo. As their personality aligned with Mo's, he stood and stated: "This is all wrong." Mo then removed all the glasses of water from the table, leaving the design as it should be used.

Terri also began to pick up on more personal information about Dawn and Ann, more specifically, about their work, as they worked together. She advised Dawn that she was starting a new role as a secretary, which was half right in fairness. Dawn was indeed starting a new role, but not as a secretary. I will not mention specifically what this role was or what Dawn and Ann do, as that was always something they preferred I did not reveal in my articles, blogs and such. Not that their career path is anything particularly untoward, simply that they worked in a role where their interest in the paranormal may be looked upon as something they perhaps should not be interested in. It always amazes me how closed minded some people are to the realms of psychical research, especially considering the vast number of academics that now look into the oddities of our world in search of answers. Still, I guess it's equally worrying that some people shy away from admitting what they are interested in because of this ignorance to the potentials of psychical research. That said, a number of ghost hunting TV shows have probably not helped that, and if anything may have hindered the acceptance process. In 2013, it would have probably been safe to say that my interest in the paranormal was the last thing I would bring up in a conversation or share with my work colleagues. I would probably even find something else interesting to remark upon when asked that fatal meeting question, "so tell us something about you that we don't know."

These days, I am thankfully more open about my psychical research interests and never shy away from discussing my favourite topic. In fact, I started a new role in 2023 and as a part of the communication to their globally located staff, they published a short piece on me and my interests in the paranormal. It was around Halloween, of course, but it was nice to be accepted for my interests rather than judged based on what some may feel is an odd or even pointless interest. In fact, as a result of that post, I have been engaged in several conversations about the paranormal at work, which is amazing. Ten years can change a lot it would seem.

As Terri provided her information to Dawn and Ann and Mo removed glasses from the table, both Nick and Peter were oddly quiet. It was soon evident why silence had fallen on the pair, as Pete was clearly showing symptoms of being in trance. His eyes were shut, but it felt as if he was glaring right at me. Rachael recognised the same thing as I did and began to make contact with the potential spirit possessing Pete, gently talking it in until it finally found its voice through Pete. Oddly and most unexpectedly, he described a great hall with food piled at least a foot high on the tables. My initial thoughts were that perhaps he was going medieval on us, but Rachael and Terri had other thoughts. She quickly asked if the floor was black and white, the answer from Pete's visitor was a simple "yes".

I quickly made the assumption that we were potentially talking to a Freemason. Rachael seemed to ask for some clarification, but none was given at this time. Pete then mentioned the name Anubis which clearly shocked Rachael. If I am honest, I was a little taken back too, as the only Anubis I knew of was the ancient Egyptian god of mummification and the afterlife. Just to be absolutely clear here, none of us suddenly believed we were talking to an ancient Egyptian god. If anything, we thought there may be some kind of message being conveyed here, but what that message may be was difficult to decipher at that point.

Then I had an idea. I asked if the table design was an old one. Pete's resident spirit replied that it was two thousand years old. My response: "Ancient then?"

"Yes," replied the spirit through Pete.

"Is the design right?" I asked.

Pete's spirit occupier said something we could not understand; it was too muffled and unrecognisable. Then he said, "Front to back, back to front!"

Oddly, this statement made some sense to me at the time, something had felt off about the layout. However, perhaps the mention of Anubis, ancient Egypt and other odd conversations may bring some perspective to it all at a later date.

The session soon came to a close after this interaction that included some additional information about some of us that Terri picked up on. We felt it appropriate to stand and engage in a short prayer, in order to close the seance. I think, given our odd visitors, Rachael and the locals desired an obvious end to the proceedings. They needed something that actually seemed to fit the whole event rather well, there needed to be structure, order and design about the whole affair. As the others moved away from the table and headed into the bar area, I remained, looking over the table, trying to process the information that we had just received.

Rachael made us all a well needed coffee, which we drank as we discussed the recent shared experience. I advised Graham Smith and the RSVP UK team that we had finished and allowed them to complete their vigil. Then I helped them pack up their equipment before heading up to bed, although my mind would not calm and continued to think about the evening's events. Sometimes I have that issue, a mind that fails to stop, calm and allow one to even sleep. It has led to me sleeping little, five to six hours sleep appears to be an abundance of sleep to me, but others may see that differently.

However, my experiences that night were not behind me, and a forgotten iPad, journal and my grandfather's pocket watch would return me to the pub's dining room, whilst everyone else slept. Oddly, the pocket watch was the main thing bothering me, something was not right and I needed to get it from downstairs. Of course, I hesitated initially, not wanting to leave my bed, but eventually I got up and headed back to the ground floor.

The door to the dining room was closed; it did not seem like the same door from earlier in the evening, I opened it and walked in. As I did so, I felt overwhelmed by emotion, it was indescribable. A troubling feeling, but equally one that appeared to raise my senses and provide an unexpected high. It was at this point that I realised that the pocket watch sat there in the centre of the table, under the jar. This was not where I had left it, but perhaps someone else had moved it after our session as we suspected that the jar may have moved at some point. I grabbed my journal and pocket watch, then headed back upstairs. There was a part of me that believed that perhaps I should not leave the table set up in this manner.

I would later talk of this experience and describe it as feeling like stepping into a railway station waiting room full of people. It was busy with conversation and activity. However, it was like being in that waiting room and being able to feel what everyone felt and hear everyone's thoughts. Of course, there was no one but me in the room and I can only convey this as a personal experience that occurred at the end of an intense night, and it could be argued that I was suffering from a lack of sleep. I can only add this experience as it is because as to date, I still have no real explanation for it.

Although my head had been in continuous thought since my return from Swanage, I had not really stopped to spend much time to write about those spiralling thoughts. So, on Wednesday, 11 September, 2013, I made my first attempt to make some sense of the events that had transpired at the Royal Oak previously.

Firstly, during his brief visit to the Royal Oak, Stewart Keeys shared the contents of a recent dream he had after I had showed him the table design. He said that in his dream he took a connecting flight from Massachusetts to Rome. There he sat around a table with Bill Clinton, Ronald Reagan and John F. Kennedy. The table was round, and they showed him a design on a normal piece of paper. This had three circles, each inside the next. At the centre was a triangle with two additional triangles to the lower left and right, between the lines of the outer most circles. The three triangles were connected by parallel lines to the centre triangle and then two parallel lines tracked upwards from the centre triangle and out of the circles. I have to admit, to me it rather looked like an upside down flex capacitor from the *Back to the Future* movie franchise. After all, it was essential in making time travel possible. However, even though scepticism was creeping in, I decided to entertain this information as sometimes you never know where it may lead and what actual meaning it may all have.

The initial connections that I made from what Keeys had outlined in his dream were relationships to potential secret societies, in particular, the Freemasons. A connection to which appears to be more widespread now than I had imagined, but I am equally considerate of how easily one can make continued connections if you allow your mind to explore every eventuality.

If I look at my family alone, as there appeared to be some obvious links to it this time around, we see several links to the Freemasons, including my own grandfather, Herbert William Knibb. The word "dragonfly" connected another family member, Pete. A friend of Rachael who would frequent the Royal Oak when he was alive was also a Freemason, as a popular local he even has a seat dedicated to him.

When we consider the table design and the need to have it aligned to the compass directions, we could stretch to see similarities here with the Masonic Lodge layout. Particular members of the Lodge are seated in specific positions, for example, the top-ranking member of the lodge sits in the East.

Odd links do not appear to end there either. Anubis came up during our seance and later I discovered that Rachael had received a small statue of Anubis from her departed friend, the Mason. When I visited Egypt, one of the only souvenirs I returned home with was a papyrus scroll of Anubis, now framed on the wall of my study at home. There are connections between Anubis and the Masons, but that may be a thread to pull on later. There are many ancient Egyptian links to Freemasonry.

It was odd back then writing about an age-old organisation that I knew little about, even though my own grandfather had been a respected member for many years. However, whilst the link to an ancient organisation such as the Freemasons was hugely appealing as a route for this case to research, as was the obvious connections to my own family, there was something that made me believe that perhaps this was not the correct direction for the investigation.

Following my return from Swanage, I looked into a number of different elements with regard to my experience at the Royal Oak. I managed to find myself heading down quite a few different rabbit holes, which can often be a slight hindrance for a paranormal investigator at the point where you try to make sense of something which makes no sense.

The connection with my own family and understanding my grandfathers became important to me. Initially, I thought them to be similar to my own spirit guides, but now I am not entirely sure that is the case. However, if I was to attribute particular spiritual roles to my grandfathers, then certainly a role of protection and strength would be given to my grandfather Len. However, my other grandfather, Herbert (the Mason), seems to be more akin to a teacher, perhaps even showing me the way on my spiritual path.

Whilst the oddities occurring at the Royal Oak may have certainly made me more aware of the more spiritual side of the paranormal and even had some influence on my own thoughts on the matter, I had to try to remain level-headed regarding the case.

Something more personal that was a direct result of my recent visit to the Royal Oak and catching up with my cousin Clare, reminded me that I needed to visit my grandmother. She was fast approaching ninety years old and as I had not been to visit her at her Cornwall home in a long time, I felt a real need to see her again. So, at the next opportunity I made my way to Cornwall for the weekend to see my cousin and grandmother. Family is important and maintaining those connections is important; my visit to the Royal Oak had highlighted that to me at least.

Chapter Six

Spiritual Circle Approach

It was becoming apparent to me that the Royal Oak was beginning to consume my thoughts, even when I was not there attempting to investigate the location. I have always been one to plan my investigations, but I have to admit I was beginning to put more thought into my visits to the Royal Oak than any other location I had attempted to investigate in the past. Sometimes the place and its obvious oddities would play on my mind at least a week prior to my visit. As I write this now and thinking about everything I have learnt, I have to wonder if potentially I had become overly hopeful that the location would deliver some kind of overwhelming evidence of the paranormal. After all, as investigators of the paranormal and researchers, we all seek that Holy Grail of evidence, but just like the true Grail, it always remains just out of reach.

On Friday, 29 November, 2013, I made an entry in my journal regarding my upcoming visit to the Royal Oak. I had a couple of ideas that I wanted to try during my visit, but in reflection these approaches seem more spiritual that scientific. I have to admit that as I read them now, I am not sure exactly what value or evidence I was hoping to gain from them. I wonder if I was simply trying to find something to do and as the approach for this visit was to lean into the spiritual circle approach, perhaps I equally decided to take a similar route.

The first thing I made a note about was a message that I wrote to Rachael in the Theban alphabet. This is a writing system used as a substitution cipher of the Latin script used by some early modern occultists. It has also become commonly known as the witches' alphabet. In more recent times it has become popular amongst those within the Wicca movement, as a form of communication. It was believed to have been first published around 1518, in a book by Johannes Trithemius called *Polygraphia* where the script was attributed to Honorius of Thebes.

I have literally no idea why I thought a message in this particular script to Rachael would be a good idea or even achieve anything. The only possible consideration I can think of is that perhaps I believed that this odd cipher might trigger something for Rachael. Especially if there was a possibility of a past life interrupting hers here. If she was channelling a spirit with knowledge of this then she may be able to tell me what it meant. I have to admit, I was not that hopeful that there would be any kind of result gained from this exercise, so I wrote her a message in the script with certainly a sceptical mind on this one.

The message would read "Twelve thirty-two fourteenth March eighteen seventy-two" and once deciphered, provide Rachael with a date. The significance of this particular date was not known to me, it was literally one that came to me during the process of thinking of something to cipher. Although, I have to admit it felt that there would be a significance to either Rachael or the investigation at some point. At this point Thomas Stevens would have been the landlord of the Royal Oak, which may hold some significance, but I cannot say what that is currently.

In reflection, writing a message in the Theban alphabet feels very much like an approach a TV show may take in order to maintain drama within its broadcast. Equally it would be something that could easily be faked to make viewers believe that Rachael had been provided a message coded in the Theban alphabet, which she would then decode to the viewers' amazement. However, Rachael has an interest in spiritual things, so we should not assume that she, like me, had not looked up such ciphers and have an understanding of them. I do not believe she did have such an understanding of this cipher, in all fairness. So, it would be interesting to see what she would make of the message, both coded and decoded.

The second idea I had for this visit to the Royal Oak was an attempt to communicate, spiritually speaking, during a seance with certain people that may be seen as having an interest in the investigation work we were attempting to do at the pub. This approach was one that I picked up from the Scole Experiment where they communicated with various characters that they called the spirit group. The idea being to create a list of people that have passed away and focus the group's attention and intention on communicating with those people. So, I decided that I would want our group to focus on the period between 1870 and 1890, as this seemed to be a time that came up during our work at the pub. It was equally the period when Thomas Stevens was at the pub.

So, my list of individuals, which was quite ambitious in reality, read as follows:

- Henry Sidgwick (31 May, 1838, to 28 August, 1900)
- Eusapia Palladino (21 January, 1854, to 16 May, 1918)
- Alexander Aksakov (27 May, 1832, to 4 January, 1903)
- Frederick Myers (6 February, 1843, to 17 January, 1901)
- John Dunne (1875 to 24 August, 1949)
- Arthur Conan Doyle (22 May, 1859, to 7 July, 1930)
- Thomas Edison (11 February, 1847, to 18 October, 1931)
- Thomas Elliot (26 September, 1888, to 4 January, 1965)
- Albert Einstein (14 March, 1879, to 18 April, 1955)
- Eleanor Sidgwick 11 March, 1845, to 10 February, 1936)

My thought process at the time was to create circumstances where we could communicate beyond the confines of the Royal Oak, disconnecting from the regular spirits that would present themselves during our time at the pub. Whilst the interactions with these local spirits was fascinating and could be understood to be a major part of this case, I was of the belief that there was more to this location and the people than this local story alone. Although, it was often difficult to separate the two, which was creating a known narrative that could begin to repeat and make it difficult to comprehend the possible psychic mediumship abilities that many of the locals involved in our investigations were displaying.

I wanted to see if the many locals displaying potential mediumship abilities could give us a little more and then help us to see that this case may be more than the location alone. Certainly, it was unusual to have so many individuals displaying psi abilities in one place or that had been to the same place, it felt that it was beyond coincidence.

On Saturday, 30 November, 2013, I made my way down to Swanage, picking up Dawn and Ann along the way. Their approach is relatively spiritual too, so would fit in well with the plan for this particular visit. As ever, the long drive along motorways and winding country roads provided plenty of time for us to discuss what we had already experienced at the Royal Oak and wonder what it may have in store for us this time around.

As ever we received a warm and friendly welcome from Rachael and other locals on our arrival, it was clear to me that this case had become more to us now; those in Swanage had become our friends and were equally curious regarding the oddities that were occurring at this old pub. Of course, from an investigation perspective I can understand the complications that building such friendships can create, but I like to think that we all had an understanding and respected each other's beliefs about the paranormal activity that was experienced. We each had varying understanding of what we thought it may be, with many of the spiritual individuals feeling it could be a haunting linked to the pub's Victorian times. At that point in time, I really did not know what to believe or conclude about this ghost story, there were many possibilities. We were looking at the potential of there being resident ghosts to various concepts of psi, like telepathy and telekinesis.

Dawn and Ann began early on by conducting some spiritual work in the garden area, using an approach where they would allow themselves to be present in the area and allow things to come to them. Oddly they picked up on a few interesting things: a burial site, which they believed to be a possible Roman grave. They also felt there was a required water feature and some other oddities, including a sword, if I am not mistaken.

Interestingly, there was a Roman grave in that area or some potential Roman remains discovered at some point in the pub's more recent history. Whether it was inspired by Dawn and Ann, there is also now a water feature and a sword in a stone in the garden. Logically one would have to denote that Rachael made the decision to build a water feature and incorporate a sword based on the information provided by Dawn and Anne. So, this would be seen as inspired rather than a precognitive event where the pair had seen what the garden may look like in the future. There is certainly a part of me now that wishes I had kept some of this stuff to myself, recorded it and not advised Rachael what they had got. That way if she went ahead in later years to create such things in the garden then we may have had some good evidence of precognition in relation to the Royal Oak pub.

Later on, Rachael, Mo and Tracy joined us and we headed up to Rachael's room to begin investigating inside the pub itself. Again, this would be a more spiritually led approach with the group utilising their connection to spirit to provide information that they felt in various locations around the pub, which may be related to its history and those that may have resided there in the past.

It was here that Mo began to advise us of some information that he was picking up on: a curved Turkish sword called a

Kilij, which was indeed a thing. A Kilij is a one-handed curved Turkish scimitar that has historical connections to Turkey. He also mentioned a water canister, similar to one you may take on an expedition, similar to an army one. Mo advised that he had to relate these items to me.

As I observed from my non-spiritual sideline, it was evident that the energy amongst the group was beginning to build. They advised that they were beginning to connect to a few spirits as we made our way around the pub slowly. The most prominent of these spirits being a grumpy old man who I assume was linked to the pub's history somehow. Mo soon connected with a rather different spirit, but one potentially connected to our grumpy old man: a young servant girl that had been abused and was most likely the mistress of the grumpy old man. The group also appeared to be picking up on the same spirits at this point, each member providing additional points to the narrative. Dawn believed the young girl to be pregnant.

It is probably important to mention at this point that the narrative that is connected to various purported haunted locations regarding a grumpy, angry or even evil male figure and an abused young servant girl mistress, is actually quite common. I remember visiting at least two to three other locations over the years where the same story has been picked up by various mediums. Does this mean that this is a common go-to for mediums in order to string together a story that we may invest in and believe as being related to the location? Potentially, this is a possibility that we must consider. However, I have been to at least one location where evidence had been found to support this story and worse still, it had ended in tragedy. The young girl had committed suicide killing herself and her unborn child.

So, there is a possibility that this particular narrative could be true of the Royal Oak too, but should we disregard it without facts to support it? I guess with much relating to the paranormal and cases such as these, we must consider the possibility and not fully rule such things out. Especially as stories like these can be buried for many years before the facts come to light. However, ten years later and still the facts have not been found, which leaves another possibility: misinterpretation of the information. That is the mediums have picked up on something but have concluded it to be one thing when in reality it relates to something entirely different. This means the story could be slightly different from this one but equally may explain some other oddities at the pub and missing facts in the documented history.

After a while Mo advised the group that we should move on as he was concerned that we were beginning to attract the incorrect kind of spirits. We moved into the next room where Mo fell into a trance-like state almost as soon as we entered.

This was an odd connection that he had established, and it really appeared as if two spirits were attempting to speak through him at the same time. One spirit appeared to make gestures with Mo's hands, whilst the other spoke of two boys around a tree and their bodies. It was very confusing, but equally fascinating to watch. However, details were lacking and it was difficult to make sense of the communication. Then without warning the communication ceased.

We then moved into the Poppy Room, but on this occasion the room was quiet and nothing was picked up. After a brief while with no connections, Rachael informed us that the room had been cleared recently and this could be why nothing had been picked up. I found this interesting on a couple of levels; firstly, the locals most likely knew of this clearing which may have had something to do with them not making a connection as they had the assumption there was nothing to connect to. A blocker if you like. However, this would not explain why Ann and Dawn picked up nothing here as well, unless this knowledge or understanding of the clearing preventing connections extended beyond those individuals' own knowledge, so that both Dawn and Ann felt they too could not connect.

It is strange to consider that something like a spiritual clearing of a particular room may hinder a medium's ability to connect to any spirits in that space. If this is to be the case, then you could equally assume that these rituals of clearance could and should work in the opposite direction too. So, such things as seances may help with such connections. Whether or not a connection has been made with the personality of someone that is no longer alive, is a question yet to be answered.

With little activity in the Poppy Room, the group headed to the twin room across the hall. At this point Mo became extremely positive and wanted to generate some good energy. So, he had us all stand in a circle and he brilliantly described the energy travelling through our chakras and bodies. It was certainly an interesting experience to be included in such a spiritual process.

It was pretty soon after this that Mo connected with the spirit of James Trim, who appeared to know a lot about how many lives we have had; I have had only two, apparently. However, as James, Mo called me Andrew. James Trim was, according to Mo or himself, from London, but the year for him was 1870. Then in the middle of this conversation with Mo as James Trim, he turned to Rachael and stated "can you concept life", then said something about parallel worlds and relativity. It was a strange conversation.

After this rather odd segment of our walk around the pub's upper floors, we decided that it would be a good point to head back down to the ground floor bar area for a break. However, we struggled to get Mo's actual personality back at that point. Weirdly, he spoke of a postcard in his mind, which I managed to interpret as a kind of call to bring him back as Mo. Rachael helped with this, helping him to disconnect the spirits and return to us. That too was a strange experience, witnessing what could be seen as the movement from one personality to another.

Once downstairs, we soon realised that the break may have been a bad idea, as the energy certainly dropped in the group and then we spent nearly an hour waiting for John to join us. This certainly lost whatever connection had been previously made, according to the spiritual members of the group.

When we finally got restarted, the connection for Mo was extremely weak, but he did provide a little additional information. He believed he connected with a powerful warrior, a mathematician from Cambridge in the 1840s and a few other lesser characters. During this communication he also provided brief details on something called Hopes Bridge, but we had little to go on in order to gain better understanding of what this was and how it might work. As Mo continued to communicate as the personality of the mathematician, he told us that he was someone called Edward, who attended Cambridge's Trinity College. Of course, both Sidgwick and Myers attended Trinity, which could be said to be a link to the individuals on my list, albeit an indirect one. Whilst these links are tenuous at best and certainly not hard evidence, they are interesting. There was apparently a Canadian that should have been on my list too according to Mo, or at least according to the Edward character.

I did briefly check the names relating to Edward as a mathematician at Trinity in the 1840s but was unable to find firm links to anyone specific. This was really a shame, as I think there was always a part of me that thought I would stumble on some character that matched that which appeared to be communicating through Mo. However, as I reflect on this possibility, we stumble on the problematic aspect that if such characters could be simply identified through a basic Google search, then you could argue that there was some fraud at play in this case. It is the more obscure information that is difficult to locate but supports these communications that becomes more valuable.

The end of our more spiritual session at the Royal Oak came to a close with Mo discussing the zodiac and making the reference to sixteen signs of the zodiac, plus additional triangles and squares, which would relate to the table design. I found this odd, as my understanding was that there were only twelve signs of the zodiac. However, a little digging later would reveal that there are many more zodiac signs out there, so this could be entirely possible. Whilst there are only twelve conventional astrological zodiac signs, there could be others related to other aspects. So, this comment of Mo's should not be ruled out, but, unfortunately, we could not explore this further as the group grew tired and its energy dropped significantly; so, we took the decision to call it a day and pack up.

It had been a fascinating time at the Royal Oak, and I had been able to witness some interesting use of spirituality and mediumship. At this point I was more comfortable with what I can only call standard ghost hunting techniques used to debunk potential activity, I knew that I was going to have to step up a little. The evening at the pub had highlighted how important this spiritual approach was, not only for the locals due to their belief, but also some of the visiting investigators in my own team that had an affiliation with these approaches. It oddly felt like an approach that was right for the Royal Oak too, and something that should not be ignored or discounted either. I would just have to work out how to balance these spiritual approaches alongside some possible more scientific or investigative methods.

During the early hours of Sunday, 1 December, 2013, I scribbled some notes in my journal, doing my best to capture some of the events of the night previously. There was a lot to remember and much of it was likely missed as it often occurred at speed and one aspect would flow into the next. It certainly was not my usual structured investigation and very much followed the path that the locals made during their own sessions.

The Theban alphabet message to Rachael was handed to her and opened after 1 a.m. on 1 December. Rachael seemed a little confused by the note to begin with, and I initially thought that perhaps it had been a bad idea. Perhaps there was a part of me deep down that for some reason thought that Rachael would instantly recognise the strange alphabet the message was written in and quickly decipher it, adding an extra layer of mystery and drama to this weird ghost story.

However, in reality, between them all and with a tiny bit of help from me, the team managed to decipher the message. Although there was not instant recognition of the alphabet, it was interesting to observe them as they worked together to crack the code. Equally, the relation that Rachael could attribute to the deciphered message was that it may have something to do with the garden wall that she had rebuilt. Obviously, this did not occur in 1872, but in more recent years.

Oddly, prior to my sending the message, I do recall Mo mentioning the Enigma code. I wondered why he may mention something like this, was it coincidence, or perhaps he foresaw the coming cipher I would provide. Is that precognition or telepathy, as it was in my mind.

As we stood in the bar area, it was discussed that the missing Canadian woman from my list may have been a Jean or Joan Simmonds or Simmons. The only Jean Simmons I could find was the famous actress who died in 2010, but there is no way to confirm this is what was meant with so little information. As such we must rule this one out due to lack of detail. Oddly, Lord Byron and Sir Walter Raleigh were also mentioned by Mo as two more possibles for my list, but I just was not sure why these may be important.

I came to the conclusion or assumption that Hopes Bridge was an equation of some kind, perhaps related to our mathematician Edward and possibly something to do with parallel universes. Closer review of my notes and various recordings had the

Hopes Bridge equation noted to be "two times the square root of seven times infinity", which may be complete rubbish for all I know as I am not a mathematician. To be fair, this was one of those statements that creates what I sometimes refer to as a "mystery loop", which is something that sparks your interest as an investigator or researcher but opens the door to a complex rabbit hole that if you are not careful, you will never find your way out of. So, sometimes it is best to not allow yourself to be sucked into such a mystery.

That does not mean you should not take note of it or consider it, but you should simply be cautious of where it may lead you, which may be far from your original goal. Again, even though this was an interesting statement, there just did not seem to be enough to go on in order to determine what it was about or what it was trying to tell us. As such I took the decision to leave it alone. Perhaps if it does mean something to someone, they could let me know.

On Thursday, 5 December, I scribbled some additional thoughts in my journal on the recent investigation at the Royal Oak. I noted that time was greatly highlighted during our time there, and what seemed like less than an hour at one point was actually closer to two hours. Now, this could simply be because we were so busy that time passed us by in a way that felt quicker than it was in reality. This is relative by all accounts, which could point loosely to the inclusion of one Albert Einstein within the list. As that is the only assumption I can draw from this, as I am sure that time did not speed up or change during our session, in order to measure such an event we would have needed a clock situated at a static point in the pub and have carried one with us, then compared the two. No such experiment occurred, and nothing was noted along these lines. Therefore, in the absence of evidence to support this I must dismiss it.

It was also some of the more philosophical sounding statements that left me thinking about the events that occurred at the Royal Oak that night. Mo stating when in trance, "Do you concept life? A cell, an action, a parallel universe?" which had me thinking deeper about the whole affair, this did not simply feel like a paranormal investigation searching for the ghosts of the Royal Oak, there seemed to be more to it. Mo also stated, "You need to just see only two lives, we only have two lives." This was something that confused me as the concept up to this point was either that there were individuals that had resided at the Royal Oak in the past returning to haunt it now or that these characters coming through in trance were past lives of some of the Royal Oak's locals. However, if the second statement was true, they only had two lives: their current one and a previous one. This concept raised many questions for me and provided the possibility that this was not the same as what we would generally consider a usual haunting of a location. All of a sudden there was a great deal to consider with regard to these hauntings. Were we looking at a haunted location, haunted individuals or perhaps a mixture of both?

Once again, a visit to the Royal Oak had left me with more questions than answers and with a great deal still to do in order to gain some kind of understanding of the oddities occurring within its walls.

Chapter Seven

The Combined Spirit-Science Approach

On Friday 21 February, I began to prepare for my next visit to the Royal Oak. This began with me speaking to my father about the box he was building for me. I wondered at times if we should be including the germanium communication device that was communicated to the Scole Group back in the nineties. This was dubbed the Trans Dimensional Communicator or TDC throughout the Scole Experiment's communications.

The original design for the TDC was received on 35mm sealed Kodachrome film. The sealed film was also locked in a wooden box to ensure that it was not tampered with during the experiment.

Speaking through the idea with my father, we believed that it could be added below the pyramid within the box but connected to the pyramid. The material that I have read on the device does seem to indicate that it could be some kind of receiver. Although, it has also been suggested that it may be some kind of beacon. Perhaps it could be both. I just thought at the time that it would be interesting to find out if it works.

I had also been reading some of F. W. H. Myers's work around this time and wanted to try and apply it to this continued investigation. This helped me to begin to think about things differently when it came to understanding how information was being communicated as often during these kinds of investigations any information that is received is believed to come directly from spirit. However, if two people can indeed communicate telepathically, which my team and I witnessed during an investigation in Royston, then it may also be possible that what we believe to be spirit communication could run along similar lines. This is where it all begins to boil down to information transference and its source. No matter whether that information is simple and could be known by anyone or the information is somewhat cryptic and potentially of greater value to the investigation, in order to understand or ensure the information as correct, someone has to verify it somehow. What is interesting is that when you start to think about the information in this way, you can begin to understand that a spirit as source is only one of many potential sources. For example, the information could be obtained through precognition, which means those who verify it or receive it will become aware of it in the future and as such are receiving it ahead of this. Then there is the possibility that the information is received telepathically from someone, or someone who believes it's from spirit but who already knows the information and would likely verify it later. Information really is a funny old thing when it comes to these kinds of oddities.

During my previous visit to Swanage, I asked Mo why he was here. Mo stated that it was because I invited him in answer to my question. Remarkably at this point Ann, Dawn and I may have got a little ahead of ourselves and believed that we were in contact with the spirit of Einstein, especially as I had attempted to use intention to invite Einstein to make contact with us. Equally, with Mo providing comments like "do you concept life, a parallel universe" whilst in a trance-like state, I was pretty convinced that Einstein had stopped by to share some insights from the great beyond. The problem is that, at the time, I guess we were blinded by the potential of connecting with the rockstar of physics to see other possibilities that were right in front of us. When Mo also mentioned Hopes Bridge as an equation, he actually started with Cambridge and Trinity College. These were possible links to Frederic Myers. As I thought about this more, I would find additional links to Myers and the founding members of the Society for Psychical Research (SPR). This included links to the Scoles Experiment and also to some of Myers's writing. At that point in time the links made sense, as I noted in my journal, but the content appeared to be attributed to the connection with Myers and SPR members. I wonder though, as I write this book, if that link was incorrectly realised, and the true source was actually me as I had all the information in my head.

At that point in time, Myers appeared to be an important character in this ongoing phenomenon; as such, I decided to ask those who would be present for this occasion to write a letter to Myers. The idea being that he would be invited, in spirit form, to join us during our session. I also asked them to prepare a few questions in sealed envelopes to facilitate this. The plan then was to open the letters after the evening's proceedings to see if there was any correlation between the events of our evening and the letters.

The more sensitive members of the group were also given some interesting characters from paranormal history to try and connect with; these were selected as follows:

Clare – Margaret Verrall
Jo – Leonora Piper
Mo – William Stainton Moses
Ann – Eusapia Palladino
Dawn – Annie Eliza
Rachael – Cora Lodencia Veronica Scott

All these characters have connections to the SPR and Myers, so the idea was that by connecting and even researching these people, the six involved would have effective memories that they would share with Myers. Having these in place may have helped to build a better stronger connection. Of course, all of this was based on belief as there was no real science behind this approach.

Still, I wanted to try what I could to ensure a better spiritual connection between the group and the other side; this approach was something my logical mind seemed to believe could be possible. Whether or not something like this could work or not really was in the hands of those taking part, as it would and did play very much on their beliefs and formed a basis for a part of the ritual or process we were associating with during our sitting.

On Monday, 3 March, 2014, I grabbed a pen, opened my journal and began to scribble down the events that had occurred on the Saturday. Since that evening at the Royal Oak, time had been against me, so writing things up had slipped a couple of days. This is never ideal from an investigators point of view, as there becomes the potential for you to mis-remember things and as such you may provide an account of the events which is not quite as accurate as we would like.

In total we had twelve people take part in this odd, combined approach, which all helped to generate a good energy and a reasonably interesting night. Present were the following: Ann, Dawn, Clare, Jo, John, Rachael, Terri, Mo, Gina, Nick, Pete and me.

As ever we began our sitting by meeting at the Royal Oak, even though we all arrived at very different times it actually worked out okay, giving us time to have a brief stint of socialising prior to the evening's events. I used to think that this helped to build the energy, bond the group, and generally make for a better circle. I even advised my team to share with the locals, who were taking part, some personal information of some kind, as this could help bring us all together. The thinking behind this being that by sharing memories, you are connecting with others, by allowing yourself to connect on that level, you are opening yourself up to allow others to connect with you. In this case it was all about bonding the local group and my group together so that they could operate well as a spiritualist circle.

I would like to think this had an impact of some kind, but the fact of the matter is that this was again based around belief and not good science. Socially speaking, those that know each other trust each other and have shared connections; they should be closer, therefore, have a deeper spiritual connection.

It was not long before the evening was very much upon us and everyone was ready to get going, apart from John, who at that point had still not arrived at the Oak. Rather than wait for him, as we really did not know when he was due, we decided to begin in a new room that had not been previously investigated. This was situated on the top floor, between the twin room and the Poppy Room. Until that evening, we had not been able to access it as it was being used by one of the pub's residents. So, we all gathered in the room and attempted to connect. Initially, some things were picked up on and it was not long before Mo slipped into trance. However, on this occasion it appeared as if a lot was attempting to come through at once, almost as if it were overloading the connection. He soon regained control and things calmed down, but it was odd to say the least. The local group decided to lead with a prayer of protection whilst holding hands. It was at this point that there was something familiar about Mo, Clare and me holding hands in a triangle, which Clare and I quickly associated with our grandfather.

Around this time Rachael also briefly slipped into trance, but it was obvious that she was not comfortable with this and quickly let it go.

At the time, Pete and Nick were stood near to the door to the room and both claimed to see movement on the hall landing under the closed door. Things were certainly picking up, as this happened a couple of times during our time in the room.

Things got particularly weird and certainly began to push that boggle factor when Jo thought that she could sense the spirit of something that was not human. She quickly followed up with the fact that she believed that this spirit had never been human. Mo followed this up by advising that he could visualise in his mind's eye a kind of lizard man walking through the room that we currently occupied. This hugely split the group in my opinion, as some pretty much accepted what he was saying as a distinct possibility, whilst others, I think, wanted to reject it as fantasy. I had heard and read about reports of lizard men spirits or actual physical lizard men in UFOlogy. They are more often referred to as reptilians and certainly seen as aliens of some kind. Cases that refer to such things, whilst rare, are not unheard of in the paranormal field. So, this isolated incident for the Royal Oak should not be totally discounted as being too much like a fantasy. I don't believe we had such a thing occur prior to this event or after, which means we may have to discount it from the wider case file.

As we began to feel that things had likely dissipated in the new room, we decided to move onto the Poppy Room and try to connect to spirit there. Whilst many of the group sat down around the double bed in the centre, Mo and I decided to remain standing close to the corner of the room. Mo slipped into trance and appeared to be some kind of clergyman. As this particular spirit, he blessed us all but appeared to take a lot longer with the process when it came to Clare. Following this, Mo changed personalities to someone we believe was called Albert Hobbs. Albert could not walk and was very tired, I helped him to sit down on the bed. During this he was a dead weight. As such, Rachael and Terri took the decision to attempt to help Albert's spirit cross over. Something I had never seen before. They held hands, Rachael held her other hand above Mo's head, as Terri advised the spirit to "head towards the light"; all of which happened relatively quickly, in my opinion.

During the group's time in the Poppy Room, Mo also took on the personality of a child spirit called Stephen, and I experienced one of the most comical trance sessions of the investigation of the Royal Oak to date. As "Stephen", Mo headed to the room's door and out onto the landing beyond it, he then locked the door behind him. We soon realised that we were locked in! As panic settled in, Mo opened the door still as "Stephen" and pulled a comical face at me as if to say "haha", which was actually quite funny. We managed to get the key from the door, but he shut it and played "peep-po" around the door a few times first. Then Terri reminded me that it was actually dangerous as Mo could fall down the stairs, so I headed out past Mo or Stephen, onto the landing to block him from falling. However, to get him back into the Poppy Room I played hide and seek with him, telling him to hide somewhere in the room.

When I returned to the Poppy Room, Mo was hiding in the corner with Terri speaking to him about the woman he was afraid of but was suddenly stopped by Rachael. Whilst Terri and Rachael spoke, I went over to Mo who was still little Stephen. I asked to speak to Mo, he replied with "you mean the man". Mo soon spoke, and I helped bring him out of trance.

We decided that this would be a good time to take a break, and as a group headed downstairs to the bar area. If memory serves me well, Rachael put on a little food for the group; and I began to set up the dining room for our sitting. I think John also turned up around this point and completed the group. Following this, most of the group also popped up to the twin room for a little while, but I remained downstairs setting up.

The group finally returned, as it seemed like I waited forever, I directed them to their seats around the room. However, for this sitting there were no designated seats, so I simply asked the group to sit where they felt comfortable. This was partly to see if the group would seat themselves randomly or if there would be some kind of significance to their positions. I am not sure there was, apart from feeling that Mo's position was incorrect.

Mo then quickly received a lot of random information which linked to the Scole Experiment, scientists and various other oddities. Then shortly after this, Mo made his apologies and headed home. Once Mo had left, I am not sure things were right, really, it felt almost as if we should end the night there and not continue without him. We did, of course, but it was not long before we moved into the bar area to try and connect.

At this point Terri felt the need to add a glass bottle to the table between us; Pete mentioned something about different types of glass that were tried when inventing the lightbulb.

After what seemed a little while when nothing really happened, Clare stated, "Is it power of the mind, or power of spirit?" Something I instantly recognised. The rest of the group attempted to approach this literally by trying to move the bottle with their minds and then asking spirit to do it for them. I did try to explain that it was a philosophical question, as in if the bottle moved then you could not prove it was spirit as it could equally have been moved by the mind or minds. This made me quickly realise that I needed to work harder to link science, spirituality and philosophy to gain a better understanding of psychical research.

Sadly, this also marked the end of our evening's investigation too, as such we called it a night and wrapped things up.

Often during the days that follow directly after an investigation at the Royal Oak, I find myself replaying the events in my mind. As the years have transpired, my journals have become an intrinsic part of the process that I utilise to help in this review methodology. They allow me to document my thoughts and capture new evolving ideas.

The investigation on Saturday, 1 March, may not have been filled with an abundance of physical activity to speak of, but it was a night of odd information that had us thinking. So, on Thursday, 6 March, 2014, I opened my journal and made some notes regarding the thoughts that were filling my head after my latest visit to the Royal Oak.

The first oddity came in the form of a message from Jo; she advised me that she had received a message which referred to the three Ts. She further advised that she believed this to relate to time, tunnel and transfer. Although, she did feel that transfer meant transport. It was an unusual message, which leaves you a little confused. However, weirdly, I do not feel it should be completely discounted. Perhaps the case of the Royal Oak could be more about time than it is about survival of bodily death.

The concept of time, tunnel and transfer was initially mentioned by Jo during our session in the dining room. During this time in the dining room, the information received or at least given by the group, appeared to relate to different years; at least that is what we believe. Oddly the years 1311, 1552, 1781, 1973 and 2173 appeared to hold some significance, but, unfortunately, we never really managed to ascertain what that was. The year 1552 was also written as 1552 x 2 at one point. What could this mean? As well as these numbers which appeared to be years, there were a few other figures too: 3, 7, 69 and 71. Again their significance is unknown to us.

One thing we must take into account when presented with such information is that whilst it appears that it should have significance, in reality it may not. These could simply be random pieces of information that we are trying to apply meaning to in order to give meaning to the sitting itself. Something I have come to notice whilst investigating is that sometimes there is just additional noise in the form of random information. Absence of meaning does not mean there is an explanation to be found; it equally could mean that there is no explanation other than that the information is random, with no meaning. As an investigator, and someone who likes to solve mysteries, accepting the fact that there may be no mystery is difficult, but sometimes as investigators we should follow the facts. If we have insufficient information to do so, then that is where we are.

Not all investigations end with a reasonable explanation or solve an age-old mystery from beyond the grave. Real life does not mirror fictional TV shows. More often than not, we leave an investigation with ten times as many questions than we had when we first arrived at a location.

Chapter Eight

The Story of the Box

As I explained in Chapter Three, the odd design that would later evolve into "the box" was something that popped into my head as I drove home on Sunday, 9 June, 2013. It was an odd experience to say the least and one that I am extremely sceptical of, to be honest. However, I found it hard to dismiss such thoughts as pure illusion, as they appeared to have meaning. Granted, they certainly did not feel like I was being spoken to by a spirit from the Royal Oak or anywhere else for that matter, but still they seemed important. Aware that ideas can also be spawned from experiences, and as such take on strange forms within our minds, I was left wondering what the hell was in my head.

Whilst this information began to dominate my thoughts as I drove along the M27, I thought it best to take a break considering how tired I was. The last thing I wanted was to have a car accident and knowing I was not fully concentrating on driving, I stopped at the next service station.

I took the opportunity to call Rachael and tell her about the strange symbolism I was receiving, and when I did things just got weirder. Rachael seemed to understand my odd description of shapes from my head, and did not question any of it. To be honest, I think I was really hoping she would question it and tell me that it was pure imagination due to my tiredness, but she did not. Perhaps her belief in what I was receiving provided me with more confidence or belief of my own, but I scribbled the design down to ensure it was not forgotten. After a brief period of rest, I switched on the engine, pulled out of the service station back onto the M27 and continued my route home.

The box itself had not quite made its way into reality at this point, but this strange symbolism would continue to enter my thoughts at various points in time, sometimes making me feel a little uncomfortable, if I am truly honest. My approach to the paranormal was always to gather the facts and analyse them with a level head. I was certainly not a medium or psychic, so receiving weird imagery left me feeling a little detached from myself. However, there was something about this particular rabbit hole that I could not leave alone, that I could not pursue; so, I allowed it to evolve naturally.

On 29 September, 2013, I wrote in my journal about the table design, as that is what I thought it was at that point in time: a design or layout for the table within a seance setting. At the time I wrote how I realised that some extra parts may simply have come from my imagination evolving this layout to find meaning; however, this was still very interesting. A square was added to define boundaries. This provided me with some possible measurements for the design or at least that is what I seemed to believe. The square would measure 50cm by 50cm; then the larger circle would have a diameter of 40cm, with the smaller ones having diameters of 10cm and 5cm. Each square sitting within the larger. I also believed that the triangles should be isosceles triangles, having two sides of equal length and two equal angles. These small details seemed to be important, but I am not entirely sure why. I was completely at odds with myself; recognising that on one hand I could simply be falling deeper down a rabbit hole that was not really anything to do with the haunting of the Royal Oak, but on the other hand believing that I needed to explore this strange path. Surely, at some point someone would point out that it's a little odd and that it was most likely just my imagination. However, as I continued down this strange path of discovery other oddities became apparent to me; one such oddity was the discovery of the "47th Problem of

Euclid" which was very much related to this strange symbolism somehow.

This strange connection to the 47th Problem of Euclid brought us back to the Freemasons once again, which for me brought more confusion. If you have never heard of the 47th Problem of Euclid it is probably because you are more familiar with its other name: Pythagorean Theorem. For many of us, school would have taught us that in a right-angled triangle, the square of the hypotenuse is equal to the sum of the squares of the other two sides. It is one of those lessons that my own children would most likely state that they would never use in the real world and as such, it is probably pointless learning. However, there is a great deal more to this than first meets the eye, especially when you apply it to the stories and secrets of the Masons. I have to admit that at this point in time, it felt as if there may be a connection to Freemasonry. So much so, that whilst in London, I even ventured to Freemasons Hall in the West End to learn a little more. The place was phenomenal and to be honest, I did feel a sense of belonging whilst there. I could understand why my grandfather was a part of this organisation. Although, I have to say that during my visit there was nothing to feed any conspiracy theories or possibilities of secret societies having a foothold at the Royal Oak. That said, there was still more to the strange connection between the Royal Oak and the Freemasons that I just could not fully quantify.

I have to admit that there were times during the investigation of the Royal Oak that I found myself tempted to explore the Masons in greater detail, and at times I certainly did. The problem was that this was one rabbit hole that would quickly become an abyss, impossible to climb out of and far too time consuming. Even when Rachael pointed out how a few local characters had direct links to the Masons, I did my best to resist the tempting secret society links.

I truly hope this was the right decision, even considering the potential that my own grandfather's spirit may have attempted to communicate with us on one occasion and that he too was a Mason. Accepting this as coincidence alone was at times very difficult and I constantly found myself questioning this link and wondering about the possibilities, but the evidence or at least the objective facts were lacking. There were certainly individuals associated with the pub both alive and dead that had links to the Masons, but little else provided us with supporting facts to take the connection beyond this point. As such the mysterious link to the Masons would dry up pretty quickly each time I thought about pursuing this line of enquiry. I had to accept that as fantastic and dramatic that it may have been, the link here to the Masons was tenuous at best and a thread I decided to leave well alone.

Nearly a month later, after the previous journal entry, could be found another entry related to the Royal Oak and this odd design. On the morning of Tuesday, 22 October, 2013, I had been woken from my usual night's sleep around 3 a.m. After the usual attempts to get back to sleep, I finally gave in to my mind which was alive with thoughts relating to the strange design. At around a quarter past five in the morning, according to the journal, I began to scribble down my thoughts. I often use my journals to download the thoughts from my cluttered and active mind onto the pages. It is a process that I have been faithful to now since 2007, and one which greatly benefits me, as thoughts processed onto a page often stop cluttering my mind or preventing me from sleeping.

On this particular occasion, I started making notes about the seven chakras, listing elements like air, water, fire, and earth. There was definitely something in my mind that was trying to draw a connection between these things and their relationship to the strange design that I had brought back from the Royal Oak. Something was certainly formulating in my mind and at the time I had no idea what it was, or if it had any relevance at all. At least making these notes in my journals appeared to help the process, and those thoughts that would not leave my mind seemed to dissipate for the moment.

Again, nearly a month later on Wednesday, 20 November, 2013, I found myself once again troubled by thoughts of this strange design, its meaning and, on this occasion, how I should progress it forward. It was becoming hugely strange and concerned me greatly; was this something truly connected to the Royal Oak, was it simply my imagination evolving an idea triggered by the Royal Oak, or worse, was I losing my mind?

However, what was really interesting was that on occasion the design certainly changed, it was no longer just a flat design to be drawn onto a table, it was now a part of a design for a box. What was stranger still, was that I had this real gut feeling that my father would build it for me. Now I have always seen my father as quite a logical man, very clever, but not someone who would believe in the crazy design of a box that his son may have had pop into his head on the way back from a ghost hunt. Strangely though, my father took on the project to build the box with little or no questions, apart from its specifications and design. This acceptance and willing to help took me by surprise if I am honest, as I was certain that he would try to convince me that it was just my imagination.

We gave it the working title of "Spirit Communication Platform"; this was, again, a feeling more than a fact and probably another strange route to take, especially as the feeling it gave me was that this box was to be a focal point of some kind for energy, generally associated with spiritual energy. The box would help to balance the focus of the energy within the group.

The box would contain a pyramid with a space below it. This provided the measurements to work with, which were hoped to be 1x1x1 royal cubit, or there about. This converts to about 52cm to 53cm, I believe. The shapes from the design and the physical box itself represent different things. The square shows boundaries, whilst triangles show balance, the circles show protection and the cross provides direction. This also includes cardinal compass points to help with that direction part too. The symbols that made their way onto the box have meaning, of course, and are a combination of alchemy and much older symbols.

Even now, as I look back through my journal at the notes and drawings associated with the box, I find myself both confused by its presence and concerned it may be from imagination alone and that it was nothing more than a huge red herring. However, no previous location to the Royal Oak or no location since, has ever provided me with such detailed and strange designs that I could not simply forget about. Both the table design and later the box design provided me with the strangest feelings towards an idea, a thought or vision, which had essentially popped into my mind, that I have never had elsewhere. This was something that I had to pursue, that I had to include and certainly had to continuously wonder about even today.

Still, building the box from these weird designs in my mind was not enough and I had to push beyond that; there would have been no point in having my father build the real thing if I didn't put it to use. That was the next step, as dark and occult linked as it now seemed, the next step was to try some kind of experiment or investigation using the box. Equally, this could only really happen at the Royal Oak, as this just seemed to feel right. So that is exactly what I did after devising a new experiment for it. Still, I would have to wait nearly six months to find out.

Six months passed before my father constructed the wooden box and it became a reality. In fact, as I look through the pages of my journals, mention of the box had pretty much ceased. I guess in some respect, I was still unsure of this odd experience, wondering if it was pure imagination fuelled by a desire to find something. There were even times that I thought the whole box thing was just my own mind's attempt to make a spiritual or supernatural connection as interesting as that of the Scole Experiment. I had to consider the possibility that there was simply a part of me wanting more from this case than was there, perhaps even allowing myself to go beyond the pure facts.

On Sunday, 4 May, 2014, I wrote in my journal and then began to put together some other information I had read in order to devise an experiment for the box at the Royal Oak. However, on this occasion I started to think more about the energy found in light itself, namely sunlight. This would mean conducting an experiment during the day rather than the night as we usually did, changing the approach somewhat. The idea was to maintain darkness in the room still but focus the sunlight by means of reflecting it around the room and into the box. However, this would mean that the experiment would have to take place in a very specific time frame. One which went beyond a simple time of day but would require the right time of year too. It was certainly an idea that I thought was good and could lead to some excellent results.

I also wondered if this odd approach would be accepted by those involved as they were all used to the usual night investigations. It is strange how night investigation has become the defined normal. I think that the only reason is the relationship to TV shows and how they dramatise the investigation process of ghost hunting. My own research into the paranormal has provided me with the knowledge that many spontaneous experiences occur during the daylight hours, rather than at night. This is why I often gather a better understanding of the frequency of paranormal events such as when and where they occur on a property. This information gives us a better understanding of when might be the optimal time to investigate. Suffice to say, it is not always when the clock strikes midnight.

So, in order to look deeper into this daytime investigation, I began to research when the sun may hit the window of the Royal Oak's Pool Room, situated at the back of the building. After some searching around the internet, I managed to find the website www.suncalc.net, which really helps you to visualise the sun's movements from when it rises to when it sets. This also includes the time it occurs too, helping me to understand when the light would hit the Pool Room's window.

Obviously and unsurprisingly, the pool table was situated in the middle of the room so the box would be placed on this at the centre. Around it would be four angled mirrors to help direct the sunlight into the box. The participating group would then situate themselves around the table equally. Ideally, we would aim for twelve people, each to be a medium or spiritually sensitive in some way. Then we would add numerous devices to attempt to monitor the environment and capture data whilst the experiment took place.

I was so focussed on making this experiment work properly that I even captured the measurements of the Pool Room, the pool table and the doorway. I think I hoped that by knowing this information would help me to create an experiment that would yield some fantastic results.

However, looking back at the words written in my journal and the ideas I had to create these odd experiments, I was missing some essential parts. In reality, I had no real reason why the experiment should be conducted as I saw it should be, or that my methodology was any different from the sensationalistic approaches of many ghost hunters that frequent supposedly haunted locations all around the world. It has no more validity than using an Electro-Magnetic Field (EMF) detector to communicate with spirits, when, in reality, you could be having a chat with an alarm system that just happens to pulse every ninety seconds. Whilst it sounds a little random, believe me I have seen this happen and then swiftly debunked it, which I think may have upset the ghost hunter in question as they thought they really had something special. Essentially though, this is another reason why we have to be really cautious that as investigators, we are aware of our surroundings and understand them in order to ensure that we are not attributing something perfectly normal to the paranormal.

Often my mind likes to devise these odd experiments to try whilst investigating, but sometimes I also have to ask myself why it may help or what could it really do. This particular experiment did have an attribute that at the time I never really considered; however, as I write this with the additional knowledge that I have managed to consume on the subject since 2014, I wonder that had I managed to complete it properly, then perhaps the results may have been better. Whilst much of the experiment, including the box, has no real bearing or relation to the case we took on to investigate, it does provide us with the potential to suspend the beliefs of many present. This is by no means proven or factual, but on several occasions during an investigation with the right rapport between those present and the correct focus on how things are done, belief that something will happen seems to creep in. A good example of this might be the Philip Experiment conducted in Canada in the 1970s where a group created a background story for a character called Philip, then proceeded to attempt to communicate with the spirit through a seance.

On Saturday, 21 June, 2014, as the summer sun brightened the UK, I made my way to Swanage. I began to wonder if using the box would yield any results at all. It would be the first time I would use the box at the Royal Oak and perhaps the first time that anyone at the pub had seen it. At the very least, it would be interesting to see their reactions to it and begin to gauge their thoughts on its use or even what it may be.

Incidentally my visit this time would follow on directly from the Summer Solstice, which appeared to have some significance to the Royal Oak as they had celebrated it greatly. So, our usual group of pub locals were slightly tired. After all, they had been awake to witness the sunrise. Although they certainly had a reasonable understanding of the ancient ritual they had taken part in, they probably did not understand the fundamental link to what is important, light and the sun, plus their intrinsic link to the energy of the Cosmos. Perhaps it is all about energy.

I arrived at the pub during the day with plenty of time to ease into the location as I did not wish to rush this experiment. I sat in the garden for a few hours chatting to Rachael prior to having a brief walk around the pub. This "walkaround" is something that I have always liked to try and do at any investigation. Whilst there is a small part of me that perhaps believes that there is a potential for something anomalous to happen or be felt during this time, the true reason for doing it is familiarisation. When investigating any location, it is always wise to conduct a brief walk around the location to ascertain the environment you are about to investigate or work with. This should even be the case for locations that you return to as things often change over time.

Following my walk around, I returned to the garden and met up with a few more members of the group for the evening. I also brought the "box" in from the car and showed it to Rachael and some of the group. Oddly Rachael and Terri believed they felt that it had its own aura, something generally associated with a person. I struggled to see this, but that does not mean it was not there. The group was certain that it had some kind of energy about it, which meant it was already doing its job. The hope being that it would become some kind of focus point for the group's energy and connections.

As ever we began our evening's investigation with a group walk around the second floor. As we did so, I wanted to try something very specific: communication by the use of table tipping. We gathered in the twin room with the group around a small table and began to communicate by asking questions. It was not long before the table tipped in response. It was believed that there may be four energies present in the room, one being a little girl. Mo slipped into trance briefly but soon returned. Then communication continued using the table to answer some pretty basic questions. It was not long before Nick also slipped into trance whilst sat in the rocking chair; it was believed he was communicating with the pub's usual resident spirits that were associated with the Royal Oak. It is important to mention that prior to Nick's episode, a large shadow was witnessed behind Nick as he stood in the doorway. The description matching a similar shadow I had also seen myself in the very same room.

Once these events had passed we moved onto the Poppy Room and attempted to connect using the table once again. This time though the table literally walked towards the door. To be clear, there were a few of us with our hands on the table as this occurred; it did not walk by itself. There was certainly a heightened amount of energy when this was taking place too, and the table felt as if it was not governed by gravitational laws, as it felt light and as if it was trying to rise up. As any investigator must, I have looked at how this may have been an instance of fraud. Is it possible that Rachael had made us believe that the table was moving, when in fact it was her? There is a great history of individuals faking table tipping and levitations, so it is certainly not a new trick. In fact, this caught the eye of many a name in the past; physicist Michael Faraday, for example, published his findings in the *Times of London* in 1853. Oliver Lodge also was said to say it was a genuine uplifting force. The phenomenon has certainly received much publication since Victorian times, but most certainly has a longer history.

Whilst at the time I was certainly intrigued by the event, I was also sceptical; tables just do not walk out of a room using the energy of those with their hands on them. Some SPR members would likely say it was pushing the boggle factor just a little. However, I had no reason to disbelieve what was occurring or suspect Rachael of fraud during this extremely weird event. At that point in time, the action of the table was attributed to the spirit that had joined us in the room and with such a physical display, how could I really disagree. However, as I write this, I may have an alternative possibility. Whilst a spirit should not be ruled out entirely, there is a possible explanation in the form of telekinesis. If this was not fraud, then perhaps the energy and movement of the table was something that we as a group unconsciously created. In fact, unconscious muscular movement or ideomotor effect, has long been associated with such phenomena. This is where individuals make involuntary movements in response to an idea. In this case perhaps the suspension of belief that allows the group to believe they are in contact with a spirit triggers the physical responses to become greater in their output. So, rather than a spirit controlling the movement of the table, it is the participants controlling the movement of the table with their minds; those on the table respond to the questions asked to the supposed spirit in the room with movements on the table. In all honesty, I am not sure which could be considered more frightening: the fact that a spirit could move a physical object so violently, or that we could move a table like that with our minds.

Shortly after this strange encounter with the table, we decided to head downstairs. The group took a well-deserved break, probably to discuss a walking table. I set up the Pool Room with the box, ready to attempt further communication with the pub's resident spirits or even some visiting ones. I have to admit, I was extremely apprehensive about how this may work or if it would work at all. Often after a significant event, like the walking table, activity at the Royal Oak would calm down to nothing. However, on the odd occasion things would actually increase.

I led the group into the Pool Room and sat them down at the cardinal direction points around the box, so each smaller group looked at one of the box's faces from their seated position. There was certainly an atmosphere in the room, perhaps the group was a little tense as this was new to them and different, and I was not sure what their expectations were. Today I would have gathered far more information from them prior to this, and after this event.

Mo led us through the more spiritual approach of opening our chakras one by one. He then passed on to Terri who took us through guided meditation, making notes to identify that we were all together. Ann, continued this, handing to me to complete the journey. I would tell them to head through the light to find themselves in the void, where there is no mass just pure energy. The idea being to allow us to disconnect from our physical existence, including our body and environment in order to create a non-physical place to work with, which I called the "lab". I described this as having a large entrance, with two columns either side of the door. This opens into a large hall with a black and white chequered floor. The hall has many doors off it, and I invite the group to search those rooms.

Granted, it was a strange approach at the time, and certainly more spiritual than scientific, but my understanding was that the group was made up of individuals that were of a spiritual belief, hence a clinical science approach would not yield any results. Hence the approach was to help them to become comfortable around the box and this environment by providing them with an approach that could allow them to relax and engage. Something I had picked up from the Scole Experiment and various other pieces of research I had read.

After a brief moment to allow the group to tune into what they were getting, I asked them to share if they were willing. Mo immediately described contact with what he described as an alien. He described a spacecraft that was triangular, but in a bubble with markings that matched that of psychic test cards: Zener cards. So, a triangle, a circle, a square, a cross, and wavy lines. He went on to discuss molecular transport or moving one solid object through another. This was without doubt somewhat strange, as it was far removed from the usual local spirits that he connects with and a new paranormal angle for the Royal Oak.

Terri described a scientist working with a book of notes, she could not see what was written though. However, she did mention balance and a large compass. Gina mentioned a room full of boxes like mine but with different markings.

The session in the Pool Room was interesting but extremely focussed. Mo closed the session by guiding us through the closing of our chakras. He helped the group to close off from this situation spiritually and, of course, safely. The group headed back into the bar area to discuss the events they had just experienced, a little like a group therapy session.

The session brought me to an immediate realisation that I should not be in the group or involved in its running. I would need to monitor the sessions and take notes, ensuring they were fully recorded, but my involvement would need to be no more than an observer. It also highlighted the real need to have the guided meditation recorded, to ensure that it was consistently delivered each time such a session ran. If this was to become a method for using the box then we needed to nail down the process precisely. Certainly, it provided focus and the group could provide some interesting experiences from it, but the question of whether this was related to the location was now a factor. Certainly, Mo's alien visualisation was not common to what we had documented previously, and I wondered whether it was his interpretation of the box or something else he had become interested in that was seeping into his unconscious mind. Either way, I found the session interesting and it certainly sparked some points to look into, but I also thought that it was removed from the location itself and its possible haunting.

Over the years, my time at the Royal Oak has continued to inspire me and further my own personal research of the paranormal. The story of the box is one part of my time at the old pub which has left me truly baffled. Even to this day, I could not fully tell you whether the strange design of triangles, squares and circles was something that my imagination created during my journey home from an evening's investigation or if it was from something within my own subconscious that needed to get out; perhaps it had a more supernatural origin that connected directly with the pub. I equally could not tell you why it felt right to evolve that original design into the box, which had some very specific measurements and hidden parts.

I have, over the years, read a few interesting pieces related to paranormal research that have talked of objects dematerialising and then reappearing elsewhere in a property, or sometimes just disappearing for good. Both the Scole Experiment and the Enfield Poltergeist case presented possible information to support that such a thing had occurred during their cases. However, the box had not simply appeared one evening, the damned thing interrupted my quiet drive home. It became something that both my father and I seemed happy to create, as if it was meant to be. And we are both individuals who would probably question most things, if not everything. The design seemed right. The measurements seemed to be right. My father bringing it into physical reality also seemed right. Perhaps it was some kind of spiritual lesson that we were both receiving or maybe it was just weird that we could not define a good reason not to create the box.

Regardless of how it was created or even why we decided to create it, the box came into existence, became a reality and a potential tool or focus point during a sitting at the Royal Oak. If I am honest, I would have liked to use it more at the location to attempt to discover what else might come from its use. Perhaps it was simply an odd looking prop, a little like a Ouija board that helped to suspend the sitters' belief just enough for them to engage in the sitting and believe that they were in touch with spirits.

So, what is the box then? Honestly, I have no idea. It could simply be a physical representation of something created originally in my imagination. In which case it really is not anything apart from a wooden box with some strange but recognisable symbols on it. After all, none of the images and symbols on the box are symbols that we have never seen before. There are four symbols that represent the elements of Earth, Air, Fire and Water. The combination of squares, circles and triangles are similar to those found in squaring the circle or, at least, they remind me of it. Squaring the circle as an expression is often associated as a metaphor for trying to do the impossible. I suppose trying to communicate with the former Victorian residents of the Royal Oak long after their death could be considered as attempting the impossible. However, the mystics saw visible events (the square) were proceeded by an invisible force (the circle). They felt the laws of the universe are ordered truths, needing understanding and to be used as guidance, which still does not take us a million miles away from the journey experienced at the pub in Swanage.

I think the box is some kind of tool or ritual piece that can allow us to focus our minds and possibly suspend our own beliefs in order to allow us to enter a different state of consciousness that allows us to engage in more supernormal abilities. Does it allow us to contact the dead and speak with spirits from the other side? That I cannot say, as I do not think I have evidence to support that possibility. Still, it should not be ruled out entirely. When I call it a ritual piece, I do not necessarily mean it is required for some kind of magic, occult or dark activity. I simply mean that I feel that it should be used within a process of some kind, all of which would enable those participating to potentially experience more. Using methods like opening chakras and guided meditation clearly had some impact during our use of the box, so that is why I feel it should be part of a ritual.

Whilst I do think that it holds some significant importance somehow, I could not tell you exactly what that is and how it works. We only helped to create it, that does not mean I know how to use the thing. Interestingly many that have seen the box or taken part in a sitting when it was used have proclaimed some kind of meaning in its presence. The thing is a challenging part of the Royal Oak case and my own personal journey within the paranormal, as it constantly makes me question it on multiple levels. There have even been times where I considered the whole thing to be my own imagination intersecting with the case and that I should completely discount it. However, it is there in its physical form now as a constant reminder of how something like this can come into being, starting simply as a thought and then through interpretation and belief, take on a form of greater importance. Not just to me, but the entire group involved with the Royal Oak case.

It is possible that the box generated a form or animism, where non-human entities such as plants, rocks, animals, rivers and even things like the wind or the sun, can possess a spiritual essence or consciousness. This could equally be extended to objects like the box and as such provide an interesting twist to the story. At first, I wondered if this could be similar to psychometry, but it did not entirely fit the understanding of psychometry which often focusses on individuals gaining information about an object's owner or its history, simply through touching it. Whilst we had explored this concept with a few of the resident spiritually gifted individuals, it had never really provided any outstanding results. However, animism appears to fit the belief-orientated oddities that were occurring at the pub.

Even today, as I write this book, my evaluation of the box sways towards it being some kind of tool we could use to suspend belief enough to tap into the extraordinary supernormal abilities of the group. I just wished I had been able to spend more time exploring that concept and learnt how to place better protocols around its use to enable some more interesting results.

Other than its use at the Royal Oak in June, 2014, I don't believe that it ever returned to the pub to be used again there. Something which is a real shame as I think it had potential to help us explore a different angle on the more traditional spiritual circle sitting, which may have provided some good results. I guess we will never really know what its potential was in reality.

Before COVID-19 changed all of our lives forever in a way that I could have never imagined occurring in my lifetime, the box was delivered to a more spiritually orientated friend of mine. Her intentions were to work with it using various spiritual methods, including crystals, to see if that would provide any insight into the meaning of this odd object. At the time, I was greatly appreciative of her efforts on what was certainly a very belief-driven endeavour. Whilst I did not entirely understand the methods that were to be used, I was interested to hear the interpretation provided by her. After all such oddly acquired information may provide us with more information than we had on such a weirdly conceived object.

However, as the pandemic approached, I lost touch with the friend, something which was entirely my own fault in reality, and something I greatly regret as the friendship had sparked some interesting paranormally orientated conversations over the years. Some of which we had even shared via the internet radio show that she used to host. The discussions on the occult, various rituals and the paranormal as a whole were often eye opening. Still to this day, though, Gef the talking mongoose remains one of the most brilliant discussions. I argued that anyone interested in the investigation of the paranormal would without doubt be interested in the investigation of the case of Gef, just as the famous ghost hunter Harry Price had been. My friend argued that she did not believe anyone would be interested in this these days. This was quickly disproved when we attended a small paranormal convention in the UK and asked a few of the people attending, including Barry Fitzgerald. All stated that they would investigate the case of a talking mongoose. It was a humorous insight into the world of the paranormal and a great piece of proof that many investigators would not turn a case down simply because it seemed completely bonkers. Sometimes you just have to take a small step beyond normal reality to gain greater understanding of the paranormal.

When our friendship drifted, she still had possession of the box and eventually I advised her that she could pass it onto one of the paranormal object museums around the country. Oddly, I did not want to retrieve the box from her, and in a way it had lost its connection with me. I felt it would be better placed somewhere else out in the paranormal world, so advising that it could be passed to a museum meant that others may see it, understand it and possibly even use it. So, without really realising it, I lost touch with a good friend and the box over the next few years. I assume that it ended up at a museum and perhaps people within the paranormal community have now seen it and begun to postulate their own theories of what it is. There is a little of me that would like to understand where it is and if it is being used within the paranormal field still. It's a little like your child growing up and leaving home to head out into the big wide world but never calling home to check in. I wish I had placed a GPS tracker and a really long-life battery inside the damned thing now to see where it actually ended up.

Sometimes I guess that we are simply not supposed to know certain things. I have no idea where the box ended up or even if it still exists, as it could have been dumped for wasting someone's space. There is a little of me that hopes it ended up somewhere and that someone has figured out a little about the idea that became a reality. If they do know something and they read this, please reach out to me and update me on the box as I would love to hear that it's still out there.

However, at this point after its interesting time at the Royal Oak, the strange object that started life as an interrupting thought as I drove home leaves the story of the Royal Oak. Although I do hope that one day it finds its way home.

Chapter Nine

The Singapore Theory Victorian Seance

On Saturday, 13 September, 2014, we were back at the Royal Oak to investigate, catch-up on and most importantly attempt to put the Singapore Theory Victorian Seance to the test. So, whilst you can always, with the best intentions, create the most detailed designs possible, often when dealing with multiple variables which include the subjects and environment of an experiment such as this, we have to make some changes as we set up. After all we are still in the infancy of developing it.

However, if the experiment was conducted in a laboratory, we may have been able to lock down these variables without having to change the design slightly to compensate. That said, this may not really be an experiment that could be conducted in a laboratory, as I believe the location itself, such as the Royal Oak on this occasion, is as important to its success. This helps with the atmosphere and suspension of belief of the sitters, allowing them to potentially accept the phenomena. This in turn allows them to possibly help to increase activity, if that is what occurs.

In this case there were some significant elements of the experiment which did not go according to plan. However, these elements have highlighted the requirement for future specifics when we try the experiment again.

We were lucky enough to have Matt and Randy from Serious Paranormal Investigations help us out with the experiment set up and monitoring at the last minute. These guys have some excellent technology that we made use of for the experiment.

The first significant change was the use of two pan and tilt cameras to help monitor the room and sitters. With these cameras, we could move the direction of the shot and even zoom in as the experiment was live. The cameras' quality was also higher than my own, which made the footage from the experiment better. This would be especially useful when a sitter went into trance because the camera could zoom in to check for any facial changes that are often associated with this activity.

Although the cameras were a significant bonus, we soon encountered our first major issue when trying to set up the devices to monitor the environment. It was my initial plan to get them as close to the round table as possible, but neither table nor environment would allow this, which meant they had to be situated on one of the side tables. The problem with this was that they were possibly too far from the epicentre of the room's activity (the round table) and thus may not be in the right place to record significant data.

In order to reduce impact on the Victorian setup, we also shielded the devices (MEL Meter [EMF & Temp], Humidity Gauge and Light Meter) so they were out of sight and also covered by another camera. However, it was there that we encountered another problem: the Light Meter we had was fitted with an auto-off function to conserve battery life. This meant it switched off minutes into the experiment. The decision was made to leave this data out of this attempt, but when we repeat it, I believe monitoring the light is significantly important.

There were a few other aspects of the experiment that I believe require addressing for next attempts too such as giving a better explanation to the sitters and guests; more active involvement and encouragement to ensure that the sitters and guests are sharing significant memories as I believe that to be vital to the success; more coverage of the socialising phase of the experiment to understand some of the psychology there prior to the seance phase.

A significant element of this experiment was control of the sitters/guests too. As understanding their location and status was imperative to the function of the experiment. However, at one point Pete (one of the sitters) left the round table and the room as he was feeling slightly odd. Although I can understand his need to leave, perhaps greater control measures should have been added for such an eventuality. Shortly after this, the pub's dog burst in and this disrupted the experiment even more. At this point, Nick (guest) took the dog out and elected not to return to the seance room. Given this situation, I joined the table until Pete returned.

This situation also left me with the thoughts that perhaps better control may have been maintained if I had led the seance element myself. Terri did an excellent job but knowing exactly what I wanted, it may have been better for me to lead. It would have also taken some pressure off Terri by allowing her to participate as a member of the group which may have improved her mediumship.

A detailed, full account of the experiment that we conducted that night can be found on my website www.ashleyknibb.com. The report on my website details everything from the theory behind this approach to what we set up and monitored, including some captured data.

As the seance began, so did the spiritual communication. Terri completed the protection for the circle and the invitation of the four spirits with a local connection and then asked if Jack Stevens was in the room. In response Mo tips his hat, it was clear that he had already slipped into trance. Terri asked for more evidence that Jack Stevens was in the room with us by mentioning the usual requests: taps, raps or knocks. Almost simultaneously, Mo slammed his fist down on the table which he followed with "encumbrance". Often, I've realised that these single words or very brief statements have greater meaning or at least that is the perception they have given in the past.

In the case of "encumbrance", it is my opinion that the sitters and guests continued with the seance without drawing attention to this word or over highlighting the fact it had been mentioned.

However, nearly five minutes later Mo left his seat and walked half way around the round table stopping behind Terri to add, "Did I mention encumbrance."

Since the experiment I have researched the meaning of the word encumbrance a little. Oddly enough, its meaning could relate to the history of the Royal Oak and the individuals we were attempting to contact. It means an impediment or burden, which could describe one of the family members who we believe may have been bed bound at the Royal Oak. Alternatively, its more legal meaning could refer to a claim against a property by another party which impacts transferability of the property. This legal meaning could also be very relevant to the Royal Oak.

Whilst still standing and overlooking the round table, Mo whispered "logical extreme". The logical extreme position is both relevant and unattainable; it has succeeded in calling the proposition into question, at least in its stated form. The question is that at this point was Mo channelling Jack Stevens still or was this statement from another? It's these smaller snippets of information that in my opinion hold more wealth as they often turn out to help link greater pieces of information. I like to think that this was a satisfactory nod to the experiment itself, but that would be a very personal perception.

At one point Terri identifies that Mo is in communication with his spirit guide, whom she identifies as a Native American. Mo also appears to channel his guide directly, at points speaking in an apparent foreign language. As they continue Mo and Terri appear to work together trying to make the communication more understandable. This includes a few actions by Mo, rubbing is hand through his hair and moving his hand in front of his face in a circular motion. After a short while, Mo looks up and tells Terri that he's okay now, but both Terri and Pete state that he is not fully out of his trance like state.

It's also at this point that Mo makes a few statements that seem to indicate that he is unaware of the events of the last few minutes. This lack of knowledge of the events that have occurred or indeed that time itself has passed has been commonplace in many of Mo's trance sessions that I have observed.

Shortly after this, both Clare and Terri identify another presence in the room. This is quickly followed by Clare acknowledging she has a spirit with her, but that she does not currently have a voice. However, she identifies the spirit as a woman and then goes on to name her as Mary Ball.

Mo rubs his face and then glances quite oddly at Clare as she states that she is Mary Ball.

Terri begins to ask Clare some questions, but communication is difficult at this time.

As this occurs, Selwyn removes his hat and places it on the table almost signifying the beginning of communication. His first statement is that he is cold. He doesn't know the spirit, but it's a male and not a member of the Stevens family. However, he does give the spirit's age at death to be twenty-two, and that the year was 1835.

It's at this point that Pete leaves the room to deal with the whimpering dog in the bar area. Although this doesn't appear to deter the current communication, it is, in my opinion, a break in the circle and in a way may not have helped.

Selwyn continues to answer Terri's questions whilst he is in what seems like a semi-trance state or at least a state of trance that isn't as in-depth as Mo's. However, the line of questioning later identifies the spirit channelled by Selwyn to be that of Davey, a stable boy at the Royal Oak. Then Selwyn speaks of how he did not like Jack Stevens, but preferred Tom Stevens. It's at this point the dog bursts into the room disrupting the sitting. Selwyn loses his connection because of this, and Nick leaves the room with Pete.

As things settle again Clare picks up on communication from Mary Ball relaying "gates" and "house gates", which appears to add an aspect of confusion. She then adds a statement which again seems a little significant: "They are a common denominator." She also states that she passed in 1860. I have to admit, as odd as it may seem, there often appears to be communication of this kind. What begins as something quite normal is then thrown into confusion by a statement that is almost out of place.

Clare continues to answer questions from both Terri and Rachael as the spirit of Mary Ball, but the answers seem to resonate with both that perhaps the spirit they are speaking with is not quite what it seems to be! A more sceptical person may simply pass this off as incorrect communication and that the information is not from a spirit at all but from the imagination of the sitter. However, the sitters present believe that this incorrect or even slightly misleading information is from a different spirit, although this spirit is not currently identified.

After about 1 a.m., communication with the spirit of Thomas Stevens is attempted and this is believed to be channelled through Peter. However, this communication lacks words and is more of an emotional transfer. Rachael focusses the questions to Pete on the garden, which begin rather basically asking what he thinks of the garden. This line of questioning soon changes though to focussing on where a body is buried, something which Pete (the spirit of Thomas) doesn't seem keen on. However, Pete does confirm a buried body and its location! Then he begins to cry about this information as it seems to have a connection to the spirit of Thomas. As Pete is crying, Rachael also reacts to this and cries too. The crying appears to cut the connection that Pete has with the spirit and thus ends communication with the probable spirit of Thomas Stevens.

Focus returns to Clare and the spirit with her, as there is definite disbelief in whether the spirit is actually Mary Ball. Rachael begins to question Clare again and soon after, Clare advises that she doesn't like the energy now and disconnects from it.

Around 1:20 a.m. Pete leaves the room to gather himself together. As there is a space at the table, I (Ashley) decide to fill it by sitting down to ensure that there are the six sitters required. In all honesty I am not sure why I did this, other than it seemed unbalanced. Once at the table, I had the sitters join hands and continue with the communication.

Mo then chips in with a conversation about Sedonia (possible spirit at the Royal Oak) and the baby. He also seems tuned into Terri, almost answering questions from Terri before she has asked them. He then gives two dates: 12 November, 1934 (12 November is my birthday), and 1957. Obviously, I was not born in 1934 or 1957. It is still interesting.

At around 01:39, Mo's focus appears to change from communicating information related to the spirits or the location and seems to focus on the individuals around the table. Beginning with Selwyn, he asks him if he requires help with the pain and advises him not to travel anywhere in three weeks' time. He then says to me, "My friend, a walk, but not a run." He then continues to speak to me: "Do you buy pencils, do you write in pencil, you need to write in pencil because of problems mistaking words." As ever a strange statement, but oddly it resonates with me as I write in a journal. He goes on to advise, "Can you look through your mind, take your eyes away and your mind will write for you." Again, another odd statement which could be related to automatic writing perhaps! Mo completes his communication with me by asking if I have a three-year-old daughter, which at the time of the experiment I didn't, but only because she had turned four earlier that year.

Directly following this communication Mo proceeds to drink multiple pints of water at speed as if he had not drunk in days. I have asked him about this and it seems that the process just appears to dehydrate him, so he simply drinks pints to quench his thirst.

Mo then goes through a few instances of disconnecting from spirit and possibly reconnecting, then remarking on the energy before finally connecting with a spirit whilst he walks around the table. Suddenly his voice changes and then he screams in what seems pain and then slowly drops to a nearby chair complaining about the pain in his legs. Others around the table get up to assist him as he drops. The locals identify the spirit with Mo as Thomas, and Pete returns to the room to hold Mo's hand. This holding of hands is to help Mo with additional energy. Mo claims that he has a "horrible energy" with him.

As we approach 02:00, Mo comments on the number of people present. Apparently 18 is too many, but we didn't count 18 in the room. However, a little extra maths revealed that there were actually 18 of us, but not all in the room. There were six at the table, two on each of the three walls, making twelve. Nick was in the bar area, that's thirteen. There were also four more in the kitchen monitoring the experiment, that's seventeen. That left one more; perhaps Mo meant the dog too! If not, then we were missing one. Perhaps the eighteenth member is in spirit?

Mo once again returns to more personal messages, firstly pulling Rachael up on her Yorkshire puddings of all things! Then he speaks to me again and asks if I am going to the jungle, something which he has said to me before, though. Oddly I do wish to go to the jungle, as I want to visit Machu Picchu. He also asks Clare if she misses her dad and remarks on him being a lovely man. He also asks Rachael if she has two names.

By 02:10, Mo has disconnected from spirit and is now getting information specific to him correct, such as his home address. Terri takes this as a good time to bring the seance to a close. She begins a prayer to close it down but loses her way and Mo chips in to help along. The seance is completed with a piece on protection to ensure all are safe.

It was an interesting session, which I cannot really say was either helped or hindered by using the Singapore Theory Victorian Seance approach. An approach which basically means you attempt to recreate events or an atmosphere that may have a connection to the location's past in order to encourage paranormal activity. Whilst we did experience a great deal of spirit communication through our local spiritual circle, I do not recall other physical phenomena, like knocking or object movement. So, it is difficult to ascertain whether it actually impacted our evening or not.

However, less than six months later I would return to the Royal Oak to give the Singapore Theory Victorian Seance another try. Possibly hoping to achieve a session that did not feel as broken and hoping for more physical phenomena for the case. Would the local spirits be willing though?

After a good journey from Hertfordshire, I arrived at the Royal Oak in Swanage at about 11:30 a.m. on Saturday, 11 April, 2015. Welcomed as ever by Rachael the landlady, I joined her and a couple of the locals for a coffee. As the Royal Oak is quite familiar to me, the next couple of hours were a kind of catch-up. The most prominent change was to the bar which had been shortened to create greater floor space. It was not long before my cousin Clare and her friend Lowena arrived at the Royal Oak. I showed them to the twin bedroom on the top floor as that would be their room for the night. I used this time to chat with the pair and also to look over a letter which I asked Lowena to write about the Royal Oak. This letter would also help her focus on the location and some of its resident spirits. The discussion was shortened as Helen, a medium and author, arrived to join our group. I invited Helen because I felt that her experience and knowledge of things spiritual would see the potential and interesting aspects within the Royal Oak. I showed her to her room which would be the Poppy Room on the top floor. I gave her some time to settle in and returned to Clare and Lowena. Shortly after Helen joined us, we headed down to the bar for a drink where we all got to know each other and discussed all things paranormal.

Towards late afternoon Gary and David arrived. I introduced them to Clare, Lowena and Helen. We then took a brief tour of the pub starting with the dining room which would be our seance room. Following dinner from the local chip shop and after more discussion, we decided to begin the evening by changing into our Victorian costumes. Once we were all ready, we headed up to the twin room to begin our investigation.

The twin room, as ever, did not disappoint. The room was quite dark at the time we entered it; the group quickly positioned themselves around the room. It wasn't long before members of the group picked up on things related to some of the resident spirits. After a little while, Helen suggested that we hold hands in a circle and focus our energy to try and attempt to manifest a spirit in the middle of the circle. Oddly this actually appeared to work. I could not make out a person; however, it was apparent that the light in the centre of the circle was darkening, almost as if its density was changing, possibly gaining mass or at least a presence.

It became apparent that the probable local spirit which appeared to be manifesting within the circle was one of the Stevens. In fact, Rachael did not identify the energy as being a good spirit. It was at this point that, for some reason, I advised David to tell the spirit what he used to do. So, at that point David announced to the spirit that he used to work as a member of the Church. Oddly at this point, everyone agreed that the spirit seemed to dissipate. However, it was later identified by Gary as pacing on the landing outside the twin room door.

We continued to work the room for a little longer connecting with some other spirits including a more timid young woman.

However, as time was ticking by, we decided to move on to the Poppy Room across the landing.

In my opinion, the Poppy Room wasn't as active as the twin room, but we did pick up on a few things including some smells which were hard to pin down; but I think we agreed on it being a medical smell. The group also felt the presence of someone and at one point a few of the group believed that they could identify the shadow of an entity.

Our time in the Poppy Room was brought to an abrupt end when Gary felt a presence on the landing. He opened the door to investigate and was met with a very solid Victorian character, this was Mo. Of course, this shocked Gary who almost dropped to the ground, something which amused the rest of us greatly. We decided to head down to the bar and take a break before heading into the main seance.

During the break, I checked the setup of the room and Gary helped by checking that the data logger was running correctly. We also checked the other items like the Stimson cube, ensuring the table and chairs were aligned with the cardinal compass directions.

Equally specific was the number of chairs placed around the table, which was twelve. This was also the number of group members for this sitting. All twelve of these individuals were somewhere on the spiritual spectrum, from slightly sensitive, to mediums and to trance mediums. It's my belief that the collective energy of all these spiritual types would assist in spiritual communication.

The plan was to begin around 10:30 p.m., but due to closing of the pub for the evening, this was delayed until closer to eleven. As we all entered the seance room I didn't think I had a specific seating layout, but it appeared that I did. I sat Mo in the North, Terri in the South, Selwyn in the East and Rachael in the West. I then sat the others in-between. Their positions also appeared to be slightly important, so it seemed. Once seated we turned out the lights, leaving only candlelight on the table. However, after a little while I felt it important to extinguish the candlelight so we would continue in almost complete darkness. We settled into the room quietly as Terri led us through protection, grounding and the opening of the chakras. This was particularly calming and truly prepared us for the rest of the sitting. The aim of this sitting was not to contact the spirits associated with the Royal Oak, but to try and establish communication with spirits that may never have been to Swanage.

When preparing on 9 April, I wrote a number of letters inviting certain individuals to join our sitting and communicate with us. These were placed on the main table next to the data logger and only displayed their first names on the envelope.

As the sitting progressed many of the group connected with spirit and relayed various pieces of information which oddly related to varying aspects of science. Most of this information could not really be related to specific individuals, or at least enough to say for certain who was being referred to at the time.

However, Terri and Mo did pick up on some slight information which could be related to John William Dunn. This was based around aircraft engineering which could be relevant because Dunn was an aeronautical engineer. This is quite a loose connection, though, but sometimes connections are.

However, what made this a little more interesting was that following the sitting Gary and David advised that there was possibly a spirit related to aeronautical engineering present at another sitting, which I wasn't present at and knew nothing about. This raises the question of was this Dunn on both occasions or perhaps another engineer?

As we continued with the sitting other spirits and information came through including a few of the local spirits; I guess it's their place. However, channelled or trance spirit communication wasn't all we experienced during the sitting. A number of the group observed light anomalies in the seance room. Members of the group pointed out several light anomalies on the chimney breast which moved around. However, during this, I believe only one other person witnessed the same light anomaly. Around the same time David witnessed a coloured light on the floor, but Gary who was sat next to him couldn't see it.

Prior to this, I witnessed an unusual light anomaly in the room. I observed what looked like a small oval light that appeared to have mass. This made it look like a kind of illuminated pebble. In fact, the light illuminated to about an inch or two out from the object. When I first saw it, it was on the floor almost close to the table. The object then moved across the floor, up the wall behind Selwyn, then across the wall so that it was on the curtain in front of the kitchen door. Although I had already pointed it out, at this point I told everyone to look, but no one could see it! I then observed the object move down, across the floor and above the table, where it rose up and disappeared as it reached the ceiling. If I hadn't observed this phenomenon myself, I might have suggested some more standard explanations. However, what I saw had good physical form as I couldn't see through it. It had a uniform shape and appeared to move at a set speed. Yet, still, I was the only one to observe it within the room.

On separate occasions and in other locations I have observed other anomalies, but they were more like white wispy smoke forms. This was very different, which is why I found it hard to accept that others in the group could not see the same as I could. The light object was so real and appeared to have physical form. I couldn't see why I was the only one that could see it, especially when it was not only in plain sight but illuminated too.

At the time, I was engulfed with confusion. How could an illuminated physical object be seen by me only? In the past I had experienced odd anomalies and more at the Winter Garden Theatre and Peterborough Museum, but on both occasions this experience had been shared with at least one other person. Even when I saw an illuminated forearm at the Royal Oak previously, in the very room where we were sat, it was shared with another member of the group. I had to question whether or not I actually saw it. Perhaps I saw it but not directly. Maybe, what I witnessed was communicated telepathically to me. Perhaps I was simply sat in the right place at the right time with the right angle to witness the phenomena.

Either way, these are anomalies that are witnessed by one or a couple of individuals, but not all at once, have raised the question of reflection and refraction being very significant to our research. The rest of the session provided more interesting scientific communication, but after a short while this diminished.

The final communication was from a local spirit that had been watching the whole thing from where he was stood behind Pete. At this point, he attempted to communicate through Pete. Pete wasn't happy with this and, with the help of the group, denied him this communication. This spirit appeared to move around the circle and try with Gary, it had been waiting, apparently. However, given how the spirit made the more sensitive members of the group feel, they advised Gary against this communication and helped to push this entity away. We felt this was an excellent time to end the sitting. Terri took us through closing the circle, and once completed, we turned the lights on.

Finally, we discussed the evening over coffee and I revealed that we may have connected with John Dunn, but the evidence was a little circumstantial at best! Often this is the case; hard evidence will elude you more often than not. Listening to the group's discussion, it certainly seemed as if all involved had enjoyed their experience and believed there had been something odd occurring in that seance room. One thing I took away was the honesty of the group which is useful in contrast to some of the experiences had. Whilst many saw light anomalies, it was rarely at the same time. There were some occasions, like mine, where someone may have been convinced that they were witnessing something strange even though others in the group did not experience the phenomenon. Others in the group remained steadfast and if they didn't see anything would state that directly, which oddly added to this mystery even more so in my opinion. Once again, I was left with philosophical questions to answer, and possibly more questions than I had arrived with originally.

Chapter Ten

Two Times Crossing Over

The Royal Oak has not only provided me with many opportunities to investigate the location, but also to attempt several different approaches to try and discover more about the oddities occurring there. So, beyond the investigations, I wanted to spend some time covering the weird ideas that evolved during the years spent at the Oak. I truly believe that it's important to be open and discuss these ideas; after all, they could highlight a better understanding of the strange experiences.

So, over these last few chapters, rather than continuing to document my visits to the pub by sharing my journal entries, I thought it may be good to discuss some of the questions that challenged me over the years visiting this purported haunted pub.

The first area, as the chapter title may suggest, is all about time. Often, over the years, whilst I have investigated various locations, the concepts related to its haunting or resident ghosts have brought about a question of time. This being based on the possibility that the reality of ghosts could be a window into another time. I am not stating this as being a fact, but want to explore it as a distinct possibility.

I am sure that in relation to some of the phenomena experienced at the Royal Oak, I would have mentioned time slips as this probably represents the simplest explanation for two times crossing over. When I talk about crossing over, this is not to be mistaken for the popular understanding of someone's spirit being stuck on Earth only to "cross over" once some wrong has been corrected. As romantically dramatic as it may seem and something that popular television shows advocate occurs often, in my experience there is little hard evidence to support it ever happening. Although this may certainly be averse to the belief systems of some spiritualists, I must follow the evidence.

When I refer to "crossing over" in relation to time, two or more, and the Royal Oak, I mean specifically points in the location's history presenting themselves in its present. Whilst the geographical location on Earth remains the same, for some reason one time appears to be slightly blended with the present. It's a strange occurrence and during my time investigating the Royal Oak, it presented itself in a few different ways.

This concept of time first became really apparent to me when a second person reported a time slip in the Poppy bedroom on the second floor. Whilst the first report of this had remarkable similarities to an alien abduction report, the individual in question was convinced it occurred in Victorian times.

As they took a nap in the Poppy Room one afternoon when they were staying at the pub, they strangely found themselves waking up to a scene more aligned with that of a hospital. They explained that there were at least a couple of people around them and by their understanding they were using some instruments to perform some kind of tests on them. Equally they were not entirely aware if they could move whilst all this was taking place. They certainly were unable to call out for help. Even though this seemed to take a while and quite a few details were shared, they could not recall how or when it all ended, and normality was resumed.

When I originally listened to this account, two things came to mind: 1) hypnopompic hallucinations, and/or 2) sleep paralysis. Even though the individual was completely convinced that what she experienced was completely real, we must understand that our minds are capable of great trickery. Not everything is what it may seem, and not all strange paranormal events are directly related to the spirits of the past. As such, we must consider other possibilities. In this case the whole thing could have been a hallucination that occurred as she began to wake up from her slumber: a hypnopompic hallucination. This could have been a dream-like state where she encountered the strange Victorian hospital scene. Whilst this may have appeared totally realistic to her, it may have only been within her own mind. Sleep paralysis would then help to explain why she could not move during this event, as this can also be connected to hallucinations.

However, on a different occasion and without prior knowledge of the previous time-related events, a visitor to the pub staying in the Poppy Room and due to take part in the Victorian seance had an experience of her own. As she stood at the room's small window, facing over the garden, she looked out beyond the garden wall and saw an orchard of trees. It was a scene that was totally incorrect for the present day, as at that point in time beyond the garden wall was a housing estate. Yet, on this occasion, what was seen was a scene similar to one that had been there in the past. At the time we made assumptions that the view was the same as Victorian times, but, in reality, all we knew was that it was a time before the houses that now occupied the space. I think the Victorian time assumption was made based on the fact that we were about to attempt a Victorian style seance that evening in Victorian attire. Still, it is another representation of a potential crossing of two times in a way that could be associated with a time slip.

The time slip phenomenon is one that often pushes the individual's belief way beyond the realms of possibility, as the experience can sound like a scene from a movie. Imagine, if you will, walking along a street, perhaps one that you had walked many times before, only to turn a familiar corner to find yourself witnessing a scene from many years previously. In many cases that I have read, the scene can be decades earlier or even a hundred years earlier, with witnesses sharing their experiences of seeing vehicles and people dressed in clothing from the 1950s and others describing their encounters with individuals dressed from Victorian times. There are other stories too from other time periods: the 1920s, 1930s, 1970s and the good old 1960s too. It is a phenomenon that leaves one in disbelief but equally has me contemplating the possibility of its occurrence.

Is it possible that these time slips were in fact more prominent examples of two times crossing over each other? Imagine for a moment that, for one reason or another, two points in time, namely one from the late 1800s and one from the present day, were close or even connected somehow. I know it sounds completely mad as a concept as we believe time to be linear, but if time and space were capable of this odd connection, then this could begin to explain both the communication experienced at the pub and even its potential haunting.

The Block Universe Theory, sometimes referred to as Externalism, suggests that the past, present and future exist simultaneously, making the forward movement of time an illusion. Everything exists in a block like a frame in a movie, but viewed from different perspectives. This concept is hard to grasp considering our current understanding of time. We are taught, as we grow up, that time flows from point A to point B, ever moving forward. Over the years that I have spent at the Royal Oak, my understanding of time has certainly been challenged in a number of ways. These potential time slips seemed as if the communication was relayed by the mediums from across time rather than from the spirits of those that once resided at the pub. In fact, I recall an odd discussion about this very subject where we postulated that there could very well be an odd scenario where our communication was also a communication experienced by those previous residents of the pub conducting something similar in their time. For example, back in the late 1800s, for some reason or another, the residents at the time, who appeared to be the Stevens family, were equally sat around a table in the pub attempting to communicate with spirits. Perhaps as they had lost a family member or friend, but given the popularity of spiritualism around that time, it is not improbable to imagine them conducting a seance. However, in some strange twist of non-linear time, maybe their efforts to communicate met ours and the connection with our mediums began.

Now, I am not stating this to be a fact; this is simply a possible theory that I wish to present in relation to the strange things that occurred at the Royal Oak pub. However, I cannot take credit in its entirety for this line of thinking when it comes to this particular case as it was Rachael herself that uttered the words "two times crossing over" during one of the sittings at the pub. With little context or meaning placed on this statement at the time, it certainly triggered the little grey cells to do their thing and provided me with much to think about.

This was especially relevant as time itself played a huge part in my investigations of the Royal Oak over the years. As you hopefully recall, time and a pocket watch were discussed in the very first chapter. My grandfather's pocket watch, which had not been working for a long time prior to the investigation, was used as a trigger object and then proceeded to start working for around twenty minutes. An action that to this day I have failed to recreate or find an explanation for, leaving me with only a potential supernatural one; whether that is power of the mind or spirit, I cannot say.

Over the years, during our investigations, time often played an annoying factor too, where we would often find ourselves missing time. For example, the investigation of a few of the upstairs rooms was thought to have taken us perhaps a couple of hours, but on returning to the bar area we would find that it was more like three or four hours that had passed. This was something that I experienced on a couple of occasions myself, when simply being at the pub during the day. Time would pass me by at rapid speed. It was odd.

Now, I am completely aware that often time itself can be an elusive animal, and our perception of time relative to the events that surround us are often incorrect. Things we enjoy doing or that consume all our focus will have time pass at what seems like a relatively faster rate. Whilst anything we need to wait for, like that time when we are at home waiting for a package to be delivered, can seem like forever. Time is relative and it can be completely understandable that time where we were focussed and to a degree enjoying ourselves, can seem to pass quicker.

However, as much as I would like to state that this obvious explanation was the case all the time, it was not at the Royal Oak and there were certainly occasions when time was playing tricks on us. At least that is what it would seem like on many occasions when we visited the old pub to further our investigations of its potential haunting.

The concept of time slips occurring at the Royal Oak on a relatively regular basis seems by all accounts something that is likely a little far-fetched and perhaps better placed in a fiction book than this one. However, sometimes the oddities of the case have allowed me to venture into theories that in the past I may never have considered, and as such learnt more about the paranormal than I had first thought I would. Prior to the Royal Oak investigations, I had never really looked into time slips but when I did, I found them to be a fascinating phenomenon, which provided a good explanation for aspects of the case. Obviously, they are not definitive answers, as we do not have that kind of proof in the paranormal just yet. While they did provide good possible answers, they failed to explain everything and those gaps meant that there must be other things going on at the pub, which meant I had to keep looking for other theories, other possible answers to the weirdness that occurred.

This would allow me to remain open minded about the paranormal possibilities that we could relate to this location and as such, I would begin to look into aspects more akin to the spiritual circle that was run from the pub by its current landlady. From these experiences, I learnt more about spiritual ideas and approaches: theories that I normally would have discarded as simple belief systems. Perhaps there was more to these past lives; maybe the spirts that we channelled could provide more answers regarding the haunting of the Royal Oak.

Chapter Eleven

Past Lives or Channelled Spirits?

Prior to beginning my investigation at the Royal Oak, I had read very little on past lives or channelled spirits. In fact, I had probably gathered more information on the subjects during brief conversations with other members of the ghost hunting community. They would share their opinions and understanding of the possibilities that could provide some answers to the oddities we were all interested in and I would listen, fascinated by the varying viewpoints of the ghost hunters. However, I was seeking something that would present itself in fact rather than those varying opinions. There needed to be something out there that could at least suggest the possibility of a past life explanation or a channelled spirit communication.

Of course, hard evidence was not likely to present in this case, after all, it's elusive in every case of phenomenon we may investigate. However, I soon discovered through the Society for Psychical Research (SPR) that there was some quite compelling research out there that may just suggest that past lives were a reality in relation to reincarnation. Dr Ian Stevenson was a psychiatrist known for his extensive research into reincarnation, where many individuals claimed to remember details from past lives. Stevenson's research documented these claims and then attempted to discover verifiable connections to real people or events. He ensured that he captured plenty of material too, with over 2500 cases captured and reviewed. Although this is not solid evidence of past lives, it does provide a large case for its possibility; especially when you consider that Stevenson also established that in some cases there were physical markings such as birthmarks which could be linked to events in the previous life.

One case that is often cited in relation to past lives is that of Jamie Leininger, who, at age two, had nightmares about a plane crash. These eventually evolved into details about the name of the aircraft carrier he was stationed on, USS Natoma Bay, his friend's name Jack Larson, and the plane that he flew. Details that were eventually verified.

This research helped me to understand that past lives could very much be a true possibility in the case of the Royal Oak. The problem would be understanding how to verify these past lives, for example, because they were related to the local area, it would be difficult to completely rule out that the information was picked up through more normal means.

However, the Royal Oak presented some oddities that slightly distorted the normal understanding of most things, as this would be similar for past lives; perhaps a reason why the term channelled spirits made more sense at times. Not only would these past lives present themselves during our seances, but on occasions they were evident in the behaviour of several of the locals. Most prominently being between Rachael and Andrew, where their treatment of each other appeared completely foreign from how they behaved generally. Then as quickly as this presented itself, it would also dissipate. This odd behaviour was witnessed by me on several occasions, but as I was not around all the time, I had to rely on Rachael to explain that it had happened in my absence. This random taking over by spirit without being invited only found one real explanation amongst the text for me: possession.

Could it be that amongst all the phenomena occurring at the Royal Oak, we could include spiritual possession of some kind too? It certainly should be a consideration for this case, but equally we should not get caught up in the sensationalism of it all. Often when we see things like this discussed on TV shows, the immediate go-to point appears to be demon possession of some kind, and that is certainly not what we are discussing here.

We must take into consideration that the spiritual circle at the Royal Oak were engaging in not only mental mediumship but also trance mediumship where they believed the consciousness of the spirits would talk through their physical person. So, it could be considered that pieces of those personalities may have remained and surfaced by themselves from time to time. And even though Andrew may not have engaged in the circles in this way, there may have been some kind of cohesion that occurred due to the time he spent at the pub, with parts of his own character seeming to connect or react in the same way that we would believe the spirits to.

So, taking into consideration the possibility of past lives and channelled spirits providing a possible explanation of the oddities occurring at the Royal Oak, the next step is to take a look at some of the spirits that have made an appearance during my time at the pub. Equally, where possible, I will attempt to establish their link to a current living local of the pub.

I would also like to state that at this time there is no evidence to support that any of the spirits' names are the spirits of the actual person that the name relates to in history. The group felt that this was the spirit they had made contact with, and I have to rely on their intuition on the matter. Whilst the information provided along with the spirit was certainly always interesting and at times the characteristics presented compelling, it would certainly be difficult to be conclusive on the matter. However, if these are the spirits of the real people, many of which existed in Victorian times, then it is strange that they may all make contact, and it does have us wonder why?

First, is the spirit of Philip Mors, who was said to be a blacksmith at the Royal Oak. In fact, the ladies' toilet was said to be his one-up-one-down cottage back in the day. What is really interesting about this particular spirit is that he is said to make contact with Terri and provides messages about things linked to the building that need fixing. Examples being the roof and a damaged pipe. In my opinion, we could all do with more spirits like Mors, especially if it helps to keep our properties in good working order.

The spirit of Thomas Stevens was said to be one of the more prominent spirits, and Rachael advised me that this spirit was linked to Andrew. Thomas was the landlord of the Royal Oak in the late 1800s.

Terri is said to be linked to the spirit of Syndonia Stevens, but I must confess in my time at the pub, I think my interactions with Syndonia were either very few, very brief or both. She certainly does come up in conversation a few times and is intrinsic to the wider story of the pub's haunting.

The 7-year-old spirit of Lizzy Stevens is said to be Syndonia's daughter and was associated to one of the locals called Kathy, but in later investigations of the Royal Oak, Kathy was mentioned less and less.

The spirit of Henry Stevens was said to be seen in his soldier's uniform by the mediums. I do not recall receiving any independent sightings of him. He was said to have been killed abroad in action.

Jack (John) Stevens's spirit, the brother of the aforementioned Thomas, was said to be linked to Roy. When I discussed his experiences with him, Roy certainly indicated some instances where he may have encountered trance mediumship and it may have been Jack that attempted to speak through him. However, as with many of these associations, these are the feelings of connection based on limited events and conclusions of the individuals and the wider group.

Pete is possibly linked to the spirit of Robert, said to be the son of Thomas and Syndonia, but certainly something I have not been able to confirm. During my time at the Royal Oak, I witnessed Pete involved in our investigations as an interested sceptical party to channelling spirits. He was also a member of the group that provided me with a tell when he was about to slip into trance. Something I did not tell him about right away to test my own theory, and which showed up each time. I missed Pete in the later investigations, after all, he was sitting there when my grandfather's pocket watch did its weird thing.

The slightly older spirit of Elizabeth, said to be the mother of Syndonia and Mary, is linked to a local woman called Chantelle. Although I take this as a given by Rachael, I do not believe I had the pleasure of experiencing Chantelle's company during one of our seances.

The spirit of Mary Ball (née Homer), who was married to John Ball and discussed in Chapter Four, is said to be linked to the landlady, Rachael. This is unsurprising really as we know that Mary would have been a landlady in her own life too. This also is potentially one of the more complex characters of this story, especially as she dodged murder, had her husband commit suicide, survived some terrible times, and took residence within the Royal Oak.

You could not have Mary Ball without her husband, which brings me to the final spirit, John Ball. A spirit that has been linked to Mo. Knowing today what I know about John Ball's story from research, I wish I had asked many more questions of Mo when he was channelling the spirit of John Ball.

There were, of course, many more spirits that came through or were said to be present over the years: the head maid, called Annie; Caroline Dix; Alice Stevens; the scruffy urchin; the young boy and girl; the governess, Elizabeth (sister of Syndonia and Mary), and many more random visitors from the spirit world. Whether these spirits were genuine connections to people from the past that relate to the Royal Oak it's hard to say, but they certainly found their way back to say their piece.

The concept of the current locals being related to people from the pub's past has been a fascinating aspect of this case. As interesting as it is, hard evidence is lacking, of course, which leaves it more in the realms of the belief of the locals. However, most seem perfectly accepting of the possibility that the spirit of one of the pub's inhabitants from the past may be partially possessing them.

Oddly, one spirit that was not mentioned in the previous list, or as being associated with anyone in particular was that of the spirit called Bernadette. A spirit that dominated our reports and investigations in the very early stages of this case. Both Andrew and Roy have had close encounters with her spirit. Encounters, which by all accounts left them terrified. My own first understanding of Bernadette was associated with the bedroom we investigated that provided access to the attic space (now a bedroom) where Pete and I sat focussed on my grandfather's pocket watch. Perhaps Bernadette had something to do with that strange event, and was trying to tell us something more.

With regard to the more dominant spirits of the Royal Oak, Rachael always advised that when certain people drank the Jack Daniel's brand of Tennessee Whiskey, they would become more open to the spirits of Thomas or John. As such, I think it was assumed that perhaps this brand of Whiskey had a relationship to the spirits in question. However, as Jack Daniel's Whiskey was not readily available on the UK market until the mid-1980s, this was an unlikely explanation. It is more likely that the Whiskey in question was either a Scotch or Irish Whiskey, which was more readily available and popular at the time, perhaps one similar to Johnnie Walker would be the better candidate here. Equally, perhaps the alcohol itself is the key, allowing the individual to become more open to spiritual take-over, allowing the consciousness of the pub's past resident to push through.

Beyond this extensive cast of local spirits at the Royal Oak, there has also been a drop in visitors, providing the case with an abundance of spiritual contact through mediumship, but also potential ghosts both local and visiting. This creates some interesting theories around whether or not ghosts are only linked to a single location and its haunting. Perhaps the Royal

Oak is a location that may act as a beacon to the spirit world, where spirits can pass through, drop in and continue on their way, similar to a train station waiting room.

Ideas around past lives, channelled spirits and how they may influence the present, troubled me throughout the Royal Oak case. Certainly, it could be said that the possibility was there based on the Stevenson research, but this focus and intensity of energy in one place seemed farfetched. However, on many occasions it presented itself to us clearly. The communications received, often through trance mediumship were completely different characters to those providing them. I have to admit, as someone trying to remain unbiased to the events occurring that it became very difficult, as, often, I would find myself whole heartedly believing what was happening. I would not simply witness the events as they unfolded, I would feel them too. Often, as information was projected through one of the locals like Mo, I would equally feel the emotion tied to that information. It was an experience that was and still is very difficult to describe.

The paranormal presents many theories regarding how certain previously unknown information may become known: telepathy, mediumship, past lives, to name just a few. As such I must accept the possibility that these were at work during the Royal Oak case. Is there a possibility of fraud, could the local spiritual circle have presented known information in order to fool us into thinking more was going on than there was? Of course, the possibility exists, and every investigator must accept that. However, throughout the ten years-plus, Rachael and the locals made no claims beyond wishing to understand the oddities; they never looked for any kind of financial benefit from the haunting and never saw it as a way to make them famous. In fact, I think it was me that suggested to Rachael that she could charge ghost hunting groups a small amount to investigate the property in order to capture additional perspectives on the haunting. And it was others in the field that suggested that the location be included for a paranormal TV show. So, basically the motive for fraud was lacking, which in my opinion makes it unlikely.

This leaves us with the possibility that the consciousness of the pub's past residents could actually be seeping into the present through its current residents. Is this to be considered just a weird phenomenon that occurs at the Royal Oak or is there an underlying reason behind this communication and this crossing of two times?

Chapter Twelve

Communication Is Perception, Perception Is Communication

An entry in my journal dated Saturday, 3 October, 2015, highlighted a strange message that I received during a session at the Royal Oak one night from Mo whilst he channelled a spirit. I scribbled some simple notes about my understanding of this odd statement, "Communication is perception, perception is communication."

At the time I thought it was simply about balance, hence the statement being almost presented like a mirror. Then I broke the statement down, highlighting the importance of communication and how it may be delivered: the spoken word, the written word and more. I even tried to look at it more philosophically. Whilst complete explanation escaped me at the time, that is not the case today.

The fact of the matter is that this phrase provides a deeply intertwined relationship between how we may perceive and how we communicate. What and how you communicate involves conveying a message, but how this message is perceived very much depends on the individuals in receipt of the message. What someone may say is often filtered through the listener's perception, which is based on their education, emotions, beliefs, cultural backgrounds, biases and more. As such, in order to effectively communicate with someone else, you must have an understanding of how your message may be perceived.

Perception itself is an active process, where people may interpret sensory information. This interpretation is a form of communication that the individual has with themselves and the world around them. It is not just what someone says to you; it is the tone of their voice and their facial expression that completes the picture.

So, communication and perception actually influence each other dynamically. And miscommunication can often occur when there is a mismatch between someone's intent and the other person's perception. Sarcasm is a great example of this, as one person's form of sarcasm may not be humorously received by another person and can sometimes be seen as offensive.

How does this relate to the Royal Oak and the paranormal? The simple answer is that spirit communication requires better understanding and perhaps at times, we got that right at the pub, but, equally, at times, I think we were way off. Often, when opening communication at the Royal Oak, like many other investigations, we would start by reaching out for anyone to connect with. However, this may not have been the best route. As we established the regular characters at the Royal Oak, learning more of their history and their general characteristics, perhaps we should have focussed on building those relationships and communications, rather than restarting each time.

Whilst a great deal of focus remained on the Stevens family as the core spirits that were both haunting the pub and communicating with the spiritual circle there, this was mostly based on the belief of those attending. I have to admit that during some sessions, the odd consciousness that would push through to the front would certainly seem like it fitted the description of a Stevens family member, especially the stronger more dominant characters like Thomas.

However, over the years with greater time to contemplate the concept of the philosophical statement "communication is perception, perception is communication", I see there is much more to be considered. If you believe that communication is taking place between yourself and the spirits of the dead, then as communicators, you need to build a rapport with those spirits;

similar to how you would establish a conversation with anyone, you may meet, by asking logical simple questions. Bearing in mind that in this situation you are communicating through a medium, who we believe is connected to the spirit. So, in this scenario, the medium acts as an interpreter for the spirit.

Still, we must also take into consideration other possibilities open to us in this strange scenario, namely, the possibility that the medium has tapped into the minds of the living. So, where we would have previously considered the information source being that of a spirit, this time we consider the source to be one or many individuals, either local or distant to the events occurring. In the seance room there may be a few sitters that have information in their minds that is accessed by the medium unknowingly. Then this information from multiple minds is accessed at the same time but creates one understanding. For example, the name may come from one person's mind, the description from another, their job from another, and their age from another, growing the full picture from multiple sources. Whilst in some circumstances this may be all the same person, it is distinctively more possible that they are parts of numerous people found amongst the living and dead, known to the group. This would help to establish a character with whom to communicate, similar to the how the Philip Experiment created a make-believe character in the 1970s. These displaced parts of potentially multiple characters create a singular contact that quickly means that information and communication is misinterpreted greatly.

The idea of whether or not human consciousness survives bodily death, and then proceeds to communicate with us from beyond the grave remains very much in question. Our perception of communication is hard to comprehend, even more so when it is considered that there are great complications with communication between the living let alone between the living and the dead.

Perhaps this is why in those cases where amazing communication occurs, it is extremely hard to accept by those that were not able to witness this. The Scole Experiment, for me, has been one such case with the claims made to be beyond belief. The mediums conveyed detailed messages, with specific characters taking on various roles as members of the spirit team. They provided various physical evidential points too, like levitating tables, various items materialising out of thin air and some rather interesting pictures appearing on undeveloped Kodak film. What is our perception in these situations, other than to believe that some higher spiritual force may be at work? Although some will have us look inward and begin to assess our own supernormal powers, perception of this communication, after all, defines whether or not we see it as the power of spirit or the power of the mind.

Epilogue

It has been fourteen years since I first investigated the Royal Oak, approaching with a sceptical mind, ready to debunk numerous claims and certainly with much less understanding of the paranormal as a whole. Like many of my investigations of that time, I was ready to visit once, gather information, and then draw conclusions before moving on to other locations, never to return. However, something changed early on for me, and the Royal Oak caught my attention. Something about that pub provided more than just unanswered questions, but a connection, a feeling, a desire to explore beyond a single night's investigation and peer beneath the surface of the place.

Time was clearly marked as important early on, connecting me to the story through my own grandfather's pocket watch, with a brief mystery for me to try and solve. However, time has not just been personal to me, it reflects the greater picture of the Royal Oak, from that dusty loft where I received a gift of mystery to the people intrinsically connected to the history of the place and its past residents. The pub's haunting is a mix of high strangeness, history and a crossroads where the past and present converge, teaching me that the unknown has not been something to solve, but a journey of understanding. A history to honour and lessons to be understood.

Whilst many ghost stories may fixate on the horrific appearance of the dead, the Royal Oak has provided so much more over the years. It is, without doubt, a storyteller describing variations of weirdness, but also tales of former residents, and at times, acting as a warning to the present owner by providing guidance for building repair, but also a place of friendship and joy. After all, I have made many a friend at the pub, who has been in my life for over a decade. This would never have occurred if it was not for the pub drawing me into its strange activity and the story it wanted to tell.

My investigations of the Royal Oak have had me change, review and reassess on many levels. The usual logical approaches have had to become balanced with more spiritual or metaphysical understandings in order to adapt to the wealth of information provided to me during my time there.

Rightly or wrongly, perhaps simply through natural progression of the investigation itself, I gained a personal connection to the pub over the years. Situations like my grandfather's pocket watch use during a sitting in a dusty loft, quickly pulled me into having an emotional connection with this location that I had not planned for and, as such, perhaps has connected me to it in a greater way. Over the years these emotional connections grew deeper through friendships and the journey I went on as a result of needing to know more, which were triggered by my interactions at the Royal Oak. My deeper interest in spiritual approaches to the paranormal came from my interactions with the spiritual circle held at the pub. This would lead me to the Society for Psychical Research and eventually a much deeper involvement with them. So, in reality, the Royal Oak pub investigations were more than me trying to understand the purported haunted activity at a Swanage pub; they were important in my own paranormal journey, something that I talked about at an SPR Annual Conference a few years back.

One thing that my investigation of the Royal Oak has really taught me over the years is that such things are about the stories and experiences of those that work and visit the pub. Whilst gathering hard data or information is always important to help prove a case, often the reality is that such things are near on impossible to establish. As such, what we as investigators find ourselves left with is anecdotal information covering those experiences. Over the years, the Royal Oak provided me with one story of a strange encounter after another, where I would have to trust the story I was told. As such, I collected them up as helpful hints about where and how to investigate the location each time I visited.

This case has some really good temporal depth to it, with much of the haunting being tied directly to the location's history. Sometimes the hauntings are supported by historical fact, but other times somewhat loosely. Over the years, this has provided an enriched narrative around the haunting that has certainly maintained my interest, as, in part, it flavours that mystery and almost provides a scenario where we begin to ask if something odd happened back then that has caused this connection through time. I recall, at one point, looking at the situation and wondering if those that inhabited the pub in the late 1800s were equally interested in spirituality and as such were reaching out into the ether, perhaps using a spirit board or a medium. In some weird twist of time, maybe they were connecting with us doing the same thing in the present day. It was certainly an out-there theory, but one that had as much possibility than any other, in my mind.

The Royal Oak has taken me from my sceptical roots in 2010 to a more open-ended exploration of the individuals, location, its history and the many stories that are tied to this haunting. There are no definitive conclusions to be provided here; the story of the Royal Oak has yet to be truly concluded and my own journey within the paranormal is very much ongoing. However, I have much to thank the Royal Oak for over the years. The friends I have made there, the people which enrich it, the warm welcome that any lonely traveller may find as they walk into the small bar area are all part of the location's true character. Its haunting is entwined within the stonework that makes up its walls, as is its history and the remnant of those that once ran the pub.

Should a haunted pub be considered a scary place to visit, perhaps, sometimes it is, yes; but in my opinion and experience, the Royal Oak became more than another haunted pub for me. It became a place of learning and somewhere to gain greater understanding of the very subject I have become so passionate about over the years: the paranormal. As such, what the Royal Oak has to offer is more than a simple haunting, it has knowledge to share, stories of experiences to be heard and a wealth of history to be discovered.

So, if you find yourself in the southern parts of England and find your way into the seaside town of Swanage, then perhaps you should find the Royal Oak and have a drink. After all, many may find a story of their own, or share one they already have, but most likely leave as a new friend of the pub. More importantly, the need to return will certainly find you, at some point, as it did me.

Timeline

My own timeline of visits to the Royal Oak stretches back to 2010 and forward to 2022 with regard to visits that included some kind of investigation. However, from 2022 to 2024, I did make a couple of visits to the pub where I sat down and had a chat with Rachael, but did not really stay long enough to conduct any kind of real investigation. It does suggest that there was still a certain pull there making me want to return to the place, even if it was for a short while simply to gain a small fix of this mystery.

Below is a brief outline of the times I visited the Royal Oak over the years, along with some other important moments.

15 March, 2010 – The first investigation of the location.

14 August, 2010 – The return investigation of the location.

9 June, 2013 – Investigation: weird table design received.

31 August, 2013 – Investigation: using the weird table design.

22 October, 2013 – The box comes to life.

30 November, 2013 – Investigation and spiritual circle approach.

1 March, 2014 – Investigation: spirit science approach.

24 March, 2014 – Trance mediumship, a greater understanding.

4 May, 2014 – Royal Oak experiment ideas.

14 May, 2014 – Some additional notes made about the haunting following medium Stewart Keeys's walk around the pub.

18 May, 2014 – Stewart Keeys's investigation of the pub.

29 May, 2014 – Capturing the measurements of the Pool Room for future experiments.

21 June, 2014 – Investigation using the box in the Pool Room.

13 September, 2014 – The Singapore Theory Victorian Seance.

19 January, 2015 – Hopes Bridge Equation and "Communication is perception, perception is communication."

11 April, 2015 – The second Singapore Theory Seance.

13 January, 2016 – Blogged about the Royal Oak as one of the top ten most haunted locations on my website.

22 July, 2016 – Spent a few days at the Royal Oak on a holiday, wrote it up on my website as a blog post about my haunted holiday.

5 March, 2017 – Joined Sage Paranormal on their investigation of the pub.

14 September, 2018 – Paranormal Lockdown UK investigation of the Royal Oak, this is when I blogged about the episode, discussing beyond their 72-hour lockdown.

28 August, 2020 – I visited the Royal Oak to attempt to gain a better understanding of what had occurred in my absence.

27 August, 2022 – Visited the pub and spoke to Rachael, COVID-19 had left the pub struggling due to some of the rules placed on public places. Equally, rising energy prices were causing issues too. Yet the activity continued to occur.

Reading back along the simple timeline, it's strange to think that over the years I did not make a huge amount of visits. Some years, I did not visit at all. However, when I think back it feels like I visited the pub on a more regular basis. It felt at times as if I was there almost all the time, but the fact is that I was not. Something, which for a long while, felt like I was going home each time I headed around the final corners leading into Swanage. And perhaps that is another reason why this place has something beyond just a haunting; perhaps that's what drew people in, keeping them coming back.

ALL THINGS PARANORMAL

Investigations, explanations and deliberations on the paranormal, supernatural, explainable or unexplainable. 6th Books seeks to give answers while nourishing the soul: whether making use of the scientific model or anecdotal and fun, but always beautifully written.

Titles cover everything within parapsychology: how to, lifestyles, alternative medicine, beliefs, myths and theories.

If you have enjoyed this book, why not tell other readers by posting a review on your preferred book site?

Recent Bestsellers from 6th Books Are:

The Scars of Eden

Paul Wallis

How do we distinguish between our ancestors' ideas of God and close encounters of an extraterrestrial kind?

Paperback: 978-1-78904-852-0 ebook: 978-1-78904-853-7

The Afterlife Unveiled

Stafford Betty

What the dead are telling us about their world!
What happens after we die? Spirits speaking through mediums know, and they want us to know.
This book unveils their world...

Paperback: 978-1-84694-496-3 ebook: 978-1-84694-926-5

Harvest: The True Story of Alien Abduction

G.L. Davies

G.L. Davies's most-terrifying investigation yet reveals one woman's terrifying ordeal of alien visitation, nightmarish visions and a prophecy of destruction on a scale never before seen in Pembrokeshire's peaceful history.

Paperback: 978-1-78904-385-3 ebook: 978-1-78904-386-0

M.E. Myself and I: Diary of a Psychic

Nicky Alan

A brutally honest journey showing strength of the human spirit, faith in the unseen and a tenacious will to survive.

Paperback: 978-1-78904-451-5 ebook: 978-1-78904-452-2

Phantoms of Christmas Past

Paul Weatherhead

True stories of seasonal ghost hoaxes and strange phantom panics from the nineteenth and early twentieth centuries.

Paperback: 978-1-80341-840-7 ebook: 978-1-80341-866-7

Spirit Release

Sue Allen

A guide to psychic attack, curses, witchcraft, spirit attachment, possession, soul retrieval, haunting, deliverance, exorcism and more, as taught at the College of Psychic Studies.

Paperback: 978-1-84694-033-0 ebook: 978-1-84694-651-6

Advanced Psychic Development

Becky Walsh

Learn how to practise as a professional, contemporary spiritual medium.

Paperback: 978-1-84694-062-0 ebook: 978-1-78099-941-8

Where After

Mariel Forde Clarke

A journey that will compel readers to view life after death in a completely different way.

Paperback: 978-1-78904-617-5 ebook: 978-1-78904-618-2

Paranormal Perspectives: One Big Box of 'Paranormal Tricks'?

John Fraser

Think Zen and the Art of Spending the Night in a Haunted House, a celebration of the dream of finding something undiscovered and different.

Paperback: 978-1-80341-524-6 ebook: 978-1-80341-532-1

Haunted: Horror of Haverfordwest

G.L. Davies

Blissful beginnings for a young couple turn into a nightmare after purchasing their dream home in Wales in 1989.

Paperback: 978-1-78535-843-2 ebook: 978-1-78535-844-9

Astral Projection Made Easy and overcoming the fear of death

Stephanie June Sorrell

From the popular Made Easy series, Astral Projection Made Easy helps to eliminate the fear of death through discussion of life beyond the physical body.

Paperback: 978-1-84694-611-0 ebook: 978-1-78099-225-9

Developing Your Supernatural Awareness

Fredrick Woodard

The common themes and details pointed out in this book will develop or enhance your understanding of our supernatural awareness and connection with our interactive universe.

Paperback: 978-1-80341-478-2 ebook: 978-1-80341-479-9

Readers of ebooks can buy or view any of these bestsellers by clicking on the live link in the title. Most titles are published in paperback and as an ebook. Paperbacks are available in traditional bookshops. Both print and ebook formats are available online.

Find more titles and sign up to our readers' newsletter at **www.6th-books.com**

Join the 6th books Facebook group at **6th Books The world of the Paranormal**